D1548470

# Building Tall

*John Hancock Center, Chicago.*

# Building Tall

## My Life *and the*
## Invention of Construction Management

### *A Memoir*

by

### *John L. Tishman*

and Tom Shachtman

The University of Michigan Press
Ann Arbor

Published by the University of Michigan Press 2011

Copyright © by John L. Tishman 2010

Published in the United States of America by

The University of Michigan Press

Manufactured in the United States of America

♾ Printed on acid-free paper

2014    2013    2012    2011    4    3    2    1

A CIP catalog record for this book is available from the British Library.

ISBN 978-0-472-11830-4 (cloth : alk. paper)

ISBN 978-0-472-02839-9 (e-book)

# Contents

# *That Day*

My office at the top of 666 Fifth Avenue in Manhattan—the same office I'd occupied since the building opened, more than 44 years earlier—faced north, so on the morning of September 11, 2001, when a colleague came in to tell me that a plane had just hit one of the towers of the World Trade Center near the southern tip of Manhattan, I left my office and went to another that faces south, where a few colleagues had gathered. From there, we were able to see the North Tower, far downtown. As with most people, I thought there had been an accident, perhaps involving a small plane; since we had served as the Construction Manager for the building of the "twin towers," I knew that they had been designed to withstand an airplane crash. One of the highlights of my career was having built the North and South Towers, then the tallest buildings in the world. And now something terrible was happening to them.

Peering through the smoke, we were horrified when a second plane crashed into the South Tower. Instantly, flames and smoke billowed from that tower as well, obscuring our view. Now we understood: this was no accident.

Unable any longer to view the towers directly, we turned to the television for information. As with all Americans, we were aghast when the towers fell. Knowing how well the towers had been constructed, we had not expected them to collapse, nor that Number 7 World Trade Center, a two million-square-foot privately owned building for which we had also served as Construction Managers, would also collapse. After the shock of their fall, we could only be

1

grateful that so many people in the buildings who had been below the points of impact of the planes had been able to get out of the buildings alive.

Over the next few days, as the details of the attacks emerged, I guess I was so shocked that I was unable to wrap my mind around the enormity of the disaster. While I felt empathy for those who had died, and for their families, and anger and sadness at what had happened, I was unnervingly calm. For several days after September 11, I went through the motions of an ordinary workday until one afternoon I found myself staring blankly at the computer screen and realized that I had been frozen in that position for hours, just gazing at the screen as though in a trance. It was only then that I understood that I had been in shock since the event.

My thoughts as I tried to climb out of that trance centered on my friend and client Larry Silverstein, the developer who had recently taken over as the landlord of the entire World Trade Center complex, and who had also developed and owned the two-million-square-foot Number 7 building.

Reporters called us because of our supervisory role in the construction of the towers, but the reporters had very little information about what happened and even less understanding of construction, so they did not ask very penetrating questions about the buildings and how they had been erected.

Away from the reporters' inquiries, some of us old hands at Tishman Construction tried to figure out for ourselves what had happened to the towers. We knew that the basic design of the towers had been sound—that soundness, for instance, was what had permitted many thousands of people to successfully get out of the towers before they collapsed—but we also realized that while the buildings had been designed to withstand the impact of a small plane, no one had foreseen that they might in the future be the targets of much larger planes deliberately full of fuel. Nonetheless it was fairly obvious what forces had been at work in the fall. The jet fuel, ignited by the impacts with the towers, had burned at an enormously high temperature, causing the steel in the buildings to soften and lose strength. Then the concrete floors, without the support that the steel had provided, simply gave way. Each floor fell downward on the next, and the cumulating floors just collapsed down and down and down until the entire building caved in under its own weight in a maelstrom of dust, glass, steel, interior partitions, furniture, and everything else that had been inside.

## Insurance Claims

In the immediate aftermath of the towers' collapse, Larry Silverstein made a claim on his insurance companies for money to rebuild, but the insurance companies disputed the circumstances of the claim. Silverstein asserted that two separate events had brought down the buildings; conversely, the insurance companies contended that the attack had been one single coordinated event, and therefore that they should be required to pay only half of the amount that Silverstein claimed to be owed.

The dispute was heading to court and would take some time to resolve, but in the interim Silverstein wanted to go ahead and plan to replace the towers. Within a few days, he called me for assistance in providing data from our building of the towers, nearly thirty years earlier. Immediately, our people began pulling out old drawings and, based on them, preparing estimates for the cost of replacing the towers and the surrounding buildings, including their interior "build outs." We were asked to supply figures based upon the original cost of all the exterior and interior elements, and from these estimates to forecast the replacement costs, which needed to factor in the escalation in prices that had occurred over the past several decades.

Complicated legal and insurance battles over the entire World Trade Center site were continuing with no quick resolution in sight, as was the painstaking clearing of the debris, particularly from the basements of the various buildings and the vast underground train station and shopping center. It became clear to everyone that nothing would happen at Ground Zero for some time.

However, since tower Number 7 had been a separate entity that Silverstein Properties had developed and owned privately, and was covered under a separate insurance policy that was not in dispute, it quickly became apparent that Silverstein was able to rebuild it. And so, one afternoon, I received a call from my old friend, Larry.

## *Number 7, and Shifting Generations*

Larry told me that he was, indeed, going to rebuild Number 7 and asked if I had a recommendation for an architect.

I did: the New York office of Skidmore Owings Merrill, with whom Tishman Construction had worked on many projects. Larry agreed with the recommendation, and we got to talking about the project.

*My old friend Larry Silverstein and I with a model
of the original Number 7 World Trade Center.*

"I hope that if you're going to start this, that we'll be able to come in as the Construction Manager from the very beginning, and certainly before the plans are drawn," I said.

"Of course," he responded.

What an opportunity!

I wanted to act quickly. The next afternoon happened to be a Friday. Larry was going to have Sabbath dinner at his daughter's home, and I rushed there with one of our standard Construction Management contracts. He and I had a quick chat, a handshake, and figuratively put our signatures on the papers, all before sundown, when the Sabbath ceremony was to begin. The final papers would wait; we both understood that Larry wanted us to manage the rebuilding of 7 World Trade Center and, first of all, to help quantify the costs of replacement to which he was entitled.

Later, Larry would tell the magazine *New York Construction*, "There was never any doubt after [the attacks of September 11] who I was going to call to rebuild. It was the most natural reaction I could have had. And they didn't hesitate either."

In the weeks and months following our handshake, Silverstein Properties held meetings at their offices, with their selected architects as well as with other technical people from their office and from outside firms. Several people from Tishman Construction went to those meetings, including my son, Dan, and myself.

After having served a half-century in the company, I had turned over everything to Dan, who was now the leader and the president of Tishman Construction. An accomplished, seasoned professional in the field, he was supervising over a billion dollars' worth of new construction in various locations around the country. But when we had done our previous job with Silverstein Properties, Dan had not been in charge, or even a top executive at Tishman Construction. Larry and his lieutenants seemed always to look to me for opinions, and never to Dan. That was understandable, since they had known me from decades of interaction on many projects, but it upset me.

*The new Number 7 World Trade Center.*

At these meetings, Dan never objected to everyone turning to me rather than to him, but I could tell that he was uncomfortable. So was I. Very uncomfortable. And not for my own sake but for Dan's: he was now the leader of the company and deserved to be recognized as such. I understood that Silverstein's people and all the old time consultants, out of the force of habit, had been looking to me for my opinions and that they did not really know Dan, who had come up in the company in the years since we had last worked with Larry. Nonetheless, because of the discomfort that I believed Dan was experiencing, I came to the conviction that there was only one thing for me to do: get out of the way.

So when the time came for the next meeting on Number 7, I found an excuse not to attend. I believed that all of the meeting's aspects would go smoothly with Dan and his colleagues in charge of providing the "Tishman input," and they did. Several times more I was invited to these pre-construction meetings, but after I had made my third excuse, the Silverstein people, the architects, and others understood what was going on, and plunged ahead with Dan and his team —and without the "old man." I felt pride that the project would continue and would be done well by Dan's team, but I also experienced a sharp sense of emotional loss at not being on the front lines as Number 7 and succeeding major projects were designed and constructed.

A few years later, when Number 7 was completed, there was a ribbon-cutting ceremony. Dan was on the platform for it and was acknowledged by Larry Silverstein and New York Governor George Pataki. I was in the crowd below the platform and away from it, content to be an onlooker. I must confess, however, that I was pleased when from the podium Larry acknowledged my presence.

Between the collapses of the Towers and the opening of Number 7, not only had that latter building been completed, but Tishman Construction had also been tapped to begin the rebuilding of the new World Trade Center. That fact astonished me: Tishman Construction would build this immense project—again! It was a measure of trust in

*My son Daniel Tishman, as he took over
the leadership of Tishman Construction.*

our company that I deeply appreciated. Also, during that relatively brief period, Dan had started to take the company up into the stratosphere, leading it to become the number one Construction Manager, as measured by the dollar volume of projects under contract.

I took satisfaction from the fact that Tishman Construction was still a private, family-owned company. Over the years, I had watched with some misgivings as our major competitors became mostly owned by foreign entities and went through many changes in leadership. We were more fortunate: Dan, a fourth-generation Tishman, was the heir to a tradition that started with my grandfather's founding of Julius Tishman Real Estate company in 1898, but that had had a rebirth when I took the company private as Tishman Construction in 1980. Our construction history included building the skylines of many cities throughout the United States of America.

# Growing Up in the Tishman Company

## My Father and His Brothers

My father, Louis Tishman, died when I just turned five, so I hardly knew him. He was the second oldest of the five sons of a Polish immigrant, Julius Tishman, who came to New York in 1885 and after running a successful dry goods business from 1890 to 1898, started Julius Tishman Real Estate. As his sons reached maturity, each joined the company. In 1914, my father graduated from Columbia University Law School and then joined the family firm. His older brother David and younger brother Alex were already there, working with their father, and so the name of the firm was then changed to Julius Tishman & Sons.

On the eve of the Great War a dozen or so such Jewish family real estate firms were constructing buildings in New York, most of the firms consisting of Eastern European immigrants and their American-born sons. It was an era of discrimination against Jews by the predominantly Protestant mainstream society in the U.S., and for these Jewish families, establishing a family-staffed real estate firm allowed them to control their destinies, to fend for themselves and to make their ways up the economic ladder. These firms called themselves "owner-builders." It was an apt and comprehensive description, since the families' stock

*My father, Louis Tishman, with his father and mother,
Julius and Hilda Tishman, in 1917.*

in trade was to acquire land, erect a structure on that property, and after the building was completed to continue to own and manage it and make income from it. This was an era in which private family businesses were the norm in American industry—well before the era of multiple large corporations and public companies.

In 1917, when the Great War began for the U.S., my father entered the military service and was sent to Europe, where he was gassed on the battlefield. Mustard gas killed about 100,000 combatants and left millions more, including my father, with lungs seriously impaired for the rest of their lives.

After the war, Louis rejoined the firm, and his two youngest brothers, Paul and Norman, also came on board when they finished their years at M.I.T. and Harvard. Paul and my father were best friends among the brothers, sharing liberal humanist interests and temperament. My father and Paul's social and political impulses, however, were 180 degrees opposite to those of David and Norman, who were politically conservative. The arrival of the younger brothers changed the alignment of the company. My father had been in charge of building management and leasing for the company until Paul arrived and took over that aspect of the business, which permitted my father to move up to directing the entire enterprise with David.

In the early 1920s, my father married Rose Foreman, who was from Chicago, and they had three children. I am the middle child and second son, born in 1926. My earliest memories are of our summer place on Lake Placid, where other Tishman uncles, aunts, and cousins often visited us.

The company's business boomed throughout the 1920s. Julius Tishman & Sons would identify potential sites for residential buildings, determine the mix and layout of apartment types that would attract tenants, and then, serving as their own contractors, would mostly erect apartment buildings on the sites. They did this successfully all over Manhattan, notably along Park Avenue. They also put up lofts and a few office buildings, often "pioneering" into territories previously thought unsuitable for the kinds of projects they imagined—for instance, they constructed the first luxury apartment buildings north of 86th Street on Park Avenue. Frequently they erected buildings before a district became fashionable, and when the area caught on they reaped the benefits.

In the late 1920s, my grandfather Julius felt confident enough about the enterprise and its future to retire, and David and my father

*My mother, father, siblings, and me in 1930. I'm on the left.*

took over the direction of the company. Concurrently, and unheard of for real estate companies at the time, they decided to take the company public in 1928, under the name of Tishman Realty & Construction Co., Inc. Part of the financing for the stock float was arranged through my mother's relatives and their friends in the Chicago banking business. It was a moment when stocks of all sorts were rising fast, and going public seemed a good way to make money. A minority of the shares were held aside and sold to the public, but the overwhelming majority of the Tishman Realty shares were divided equally among the five brothers, each receiving 20 percent. Tishman Realty became a public firm controlled by the family stock ownership.

The years 1929 and 1930 were the most successful in the company's business history; in 1930, they completed six apartment buildings and rented every unit in them all.

In 1931, the mustard gas that had weakened my father's constitution spawned cancer that made him gravely ill. My only knowledge of this was that I occasionally saw him in his bed being treated for something—I had no sense of what that might be. A nurse and my mother were always at his bedside. One of my only recollections of my father is of the moment that from his bed he gave me a grape lollipop. During his final days, I was sent to the Carlyle Hotel with my eight-month-old sister, Louise, and her nurse. About a week later, my mother came to the hotel and told me that my father had passed on. I had just turned five.

## School, Navy, Teaching

After my father's death, my mother, my siblings and I continued to live in Tishman-owned buildings. Still young, I was unaware of the Depression that engulfed the entire country and that seriously impacted the real estate business. For income, my mother had money from the substantial life insurance that my father had been prescient enough to buy.

At three-and-a-half, I had entered the Walden School, which my parents chose because it embodied their progressive ideas. Walden was coeducational, multicultural, and very progressive, certainly when compared to the more establishment-type private prep schools attended by my cousins. In the 1930s, many of the Walden teachers were refugees from Nazi Germany. Their husbands and wives were professors at The New School, in Greenwich Village, a hotbed of intellectualism and liberal thought. My mother was as progressive as they were. I remember at an early age picketing General Electric with teachers and classmates, though I cannot recall what we were picketing for or against.

During the school year we four lived in a Tishman property, a four-story walk-up brownstone on 72nd Street between Second and Third Avenues. Later I would learn that this building had been purchased as a "light protector," a small building on a lot that was next to a larger and taller apartment building; the firm had purchased it so that another developer could not come in and erect a tall building on that lot and block the light coming into the Tishman apartment building's windows. "You'll be happier in a Tishman building," was the slogan of the ads the company placed in newspapers and in *Playbill*, a magazine distributed in theaters. Sunlight coming through the windows was considered a contributor to that happiness and a necessity for good apartment layouts.

Summers we four spent at the very large "summer camp" that my father had designed and built on Lake Placid. My dad had the opportunity to live in it only one summer, but after he died we summered there for many years. Occasionally other Tishmans would descend on us and "share" our house as my mother's guests. I remember listening to a Franklin Roosevelt fireside chat there in 1933 or 1934—gathered around a large radio in the living room with Uncle David, his wife, Anne, and their three children, my cousins Bob, Alan, and Virginia. As the president spoke, David became visibly and volubly angry. My mother, a liberal Democrat, was uncomfortable at this rude behavior from a guest in her house. I also was upset at anyone saying bad things about my president, particularly since Roosevelt had come to Lake Placid to open and inaugurate the road up Whiteface Mountain. The local man in charge of that toll road, whose son was our caretaker, had invited us to attend that ceremony.

Fatherless, in those days I gravitated to surrogate fathers such as our caretaker, especially during the long summers at Lake Placid. I also had pretty free rein to use the lake, and permission to drive the small outboard engine on our tub-shaped boat, *Leviathan*. I would take every opportunity to run it to the public boat landing, using such excuses as that the engine needed gas, and then I would hang around the boat landing, helping out the guys who were taking care of the speedboats belonging to the various houses around the lake. After a while, at the landing, I was given the opportunity to help out on the *Doris*, the tour boat. The largest vessel on the lake, it also served as the mail boat for the houses on the islands and for distant homes that were not reachable by road. Each day, the *Doris* made three trips around the lake, carrying as many as 70 tourists on each run. As a mail boat, it would slide by long docks protruding from each house, and we would exchange a bag of incoming mail for a few pieces of outgoing mail in an otherwise empty mailbag that someone from the house would hold out for us to grab as we brushed by the dock without stopping.

Captain Stevens let me steer and perform other duties, which made me feel very important. He too was one of my substitute fathers. I took my duties on board seriously, in part because the captain paid me handsomely, allowing me free access to the candy drawer that was normally used as a profit center, from which I would sell candy to the tourists as they rode around the lake.

Another substitute father was an electrical engineer named Otto Friend, whose son, Jerry, was my best pal at Walden.

I did reasonably well in school despite having what I would later learn was dyslexia; fortunately for me, Walden allowed me to develop what skills I had and did not force me to conform to the sort of traditional educational standards that are based on reading proficiency. For a dyslexic, it is next to impossible to perform at the reading level that others are routinely expected to reach.

Lacking a father's direction or a male mentor to specifically guide me, I had no idea what field I ought to study in college, or where I should go to study. But Jerry Friend, a fellow student, was heading to Michigan, his father's alma mater, to become an electrical engineer, as his father had. I decided that was what I would do as well, so I applied and was accepted.

I was 16, and began at Michigan a week after my high school graduation because World War II was already in progress and young men were expected to rush through their education so they could then do their military service. At Michigan, I also joined the V-12 program for future Navy officers, although I had to wait to do so until I'd turned 18 and was eligible. I took to engineering pretty well, learning various aspects of it and concentrating on electrical engineering. In college, I read my first book, a novel; before that, I'd gotten by in essay questions on required books because I'd read the flap copy and other clues to content, and had based my written answers on those shortcuts. Mathematics was easier for me, and engineering had lots of math.

In the spring of 1945, two terrible events occurred. Jerry Friend was killed. He had wanted to join the Navy but had not been accepted, since he was colorblind; instead, he had joined the Army Corps of Engineers, but never got into their Officer Candidate School because after basic training he was immediately sent to the European battle-field. After the Allies had lost ground in the Battle of the Bulge, in early March 1945, they crossed again into Germany at the Remagen Bridge. Jerry was one of the first to cross that bridge, and was killed while attempting to disable a mine. His death left a big hole in my life. As I was still trying to come to terms with it, President Roosevelt died suddenly on April 12, 1945. His death also hit me hard.

The war ended before I graduated college in early 1946. The engineering program had taken me two years and seven months. I had just turned nineteen. On graduation day, there were dual ceremonies; in the first, I received my college diploma, and in the second, my commission as an ensign in the Navy. I was equally proud of both.

My own service duty was without hazard. With a complement of other junior officers from various colleges, I took training at Newport, Rhode Island and was then stationed aboard the *U.S.S. Columbia*, a light cruiser that had served for years in the Pacific, had been hit by a kamikaze plane, and was now on the verge of being retired. When we went on board we were asked about our hobbies. I put down photography and was promptly named the ship's photographic officer. We steamed up and down the East Coast, and the Caribbean, and even along the St. Lawrence River for a ceremony in Quebec. At the various ports, we participated in parades and reviews, accepting accolades from the public that were really tributes to the sailors who had actually fought aboard the *Columbia* in the war. Later I'd joke about my combat experience in the "Battle of Bermuda."

Emerging from the service, I had no idea of what to do for a career or how to earn a living. Since my father was long gone, I had no knowledge or real connection to the Tishman Realty firm, and no interest in it. One day I visited Walden to see my high school teacher and friends. On that day, the regular high school math teacher called in, saying he had pink eye, a highly infectious conjunctivitis, and I was drafted to take over his classes for a spell. Shortly, when it became clear that the math teacher was not going to return to his post, I was asked to stay on for a year as the high school math teacher.

I liked teaching and discovered that I was pretty good at it. I developed a new friend in fellow instructor Hans Maeder, who taught German and European History at Walden. Maeder, whose German accent was quite thick, was a refugee from Nazi Germany, albeit not a Jewish one. He had led an anti-Hitler youth group and later had been hidden from the Nazis by a Dutch family. He escaped to South Africa, and taught there and in the Philippines before coming to the U.S.

On weekends, Hans and I would take the Walden juniors and seniors camping near Croton, north of New York City, along the Hudson River. During my time at Walden, Hans was appointed director of the school, but he really wanted to start a school of his own. Some teachers from Johns Hopkins had tried to start a school in the Berkshires, but had been unable to do so. Hans and his wife, Ruth, bought

*Ensign in the U.S. Navy, 1946.*

the old Mark Hanna estate in Interlaken, Massachusetts, and in 1949 began the Stockbridge School. Almost every weekend I would come up to help, and also assisted with arranging the financing for them to purchase the estate and then supervised the construction of a dormitory. The school was coeducational, interracial, interdenominational, multicultural, and international in outlook. We flew the United Nations flag above the American flag, which upset the local people, although it was then specifically encouraged and was certainly not against the law. All of this was quite unusual for prep schools in that era.

## Going to the Company

During my childhood, and while I was teaching at Walden School, my favorite uncle was Paul, a sophisticated man of many interests. He and I shared several tastes—photography, woodworking, and raising pure-bred dogs; he was also assembling very fine collections of African and Peruvian art, almost unheard of in America in the 1940s. Paul's photographs were artworks themselves; several were used in major product advertising campaigns. Paul did things to a fare-thee-well, getting deeply involved in every subject he touched, for instance becoming an expert in the cultures whose art he collected. He was also extremely progressive in his politics, as my mother and I were.

My mother came by her sympathies naturally. She and all of her close Chicago friends leaned to the left in political terms. My mother and Ruth Tishman, Paul's wife, also quite liberal in politics, were the antithesis of the other women in the Tishman clan in that and in many other ways; my mother's and Ruth's interests, values, and sets of friends set them dramatically apart from those of the other Tishman women.

After I'd been teaching for two years, Uncle David suggested to me that I come into the Tishman Realty & Construction firm, as all my male cousins were doing.

I was hesitant to stop teaching, as I loved doing it. But Hans Maeder urged me to go, so I agreed. I also hoped that in moving to the real estate firm, I'd be joining my favorite uncle, Paul, although he said nothing to me one way or another about joining the family firm, for reasons that I would soon discover.

When I look back on the circumstances of my joining the firm in 1947, I believe my uncles had two reasons for bringing me in. The first was the family culture; all Tishman males were expected to become part of the company. The exception was my older brother; he had graduated Johns Hopkins, but his physical and mental difficulties kept him from full-time employment. Their second reason was that perhaps my engineering background would be of assistance to them in construction. After a long period of Depression and war, the real estate business was finally booming again, and Tishman Realty had many projects waiting to be built, owned, and managed.

As soon as I joined the family firm, I discovered that Paul, my favorite uncle, was no longer on the premises. I was told that he was on medical leave but was expected back at some unspecified time. I later learned that he had taken a leave to undergo psychoanalysis—something in which he believed, although his brothers did not—and to re-evaluate his future course in life. The combination would soon cause him to resign from the family firm and to begin his own general contracting firm. To state it simply: Paul liked construction but had decided that he could no longer work well with his oldest and youngest brothers, David and Norman—and so he had gone out on his own.

## Nine Tishmans

When I joined the family firm, there were seven other Tishmans on the roster: my uncles David, Norman, and Alex; David's sons Bob and Alan; and Alex's sons Edward and Bill. Later, Norman's son Peter joined, which made nine Tishmans. As if that was not complicated enough, David and Norman were married to sisters.

The company, I very quickly discovered, was completely hierarchical. Oldest brother David was the boss, and it was understood that he was shortly to yield control to his youngest brother, Norman. In 1948, David became chairman of the board and Norman became president of the firm. It was presumed that after Norman retired—something not expected to happen anytime soon—the leader would be the oldest of the cousins, David's oldest son, Bob, who was a decade older than me. My youngest cousin, Peter, was a decade younger than I was and twenty years younger than Bob.

Tishman Realty was organized more or less in three parts. When I joined, David, Norman, and Bob handled the acquisition of properties, financing, and the like—what today we'd call real estate development. Norman was also involved, with my cousin Alan, in the leasing and management of the Tishman-owned properties; it was understood that when Norman became the overall boss, Alan would completely take over leasing and management.

Construction was third division, and it was somewhat of a stepchild. Alex was nominally in charge of construction—that had been Paul's bailiwick, but Paul was now gone. Neither Norman nor David had much of an interest in or grasp of construction. Norman found it distasteful and dirty; for instance, when the company was building 460 Park Avenue, which was to be our headquarters for a decade, Norman made sure that when bankers and executives would get off the elevator they would enter our headquarters from one grand door, while the dirty-booted would be required to enter through a second door. The people wearing dust-covered boots—subcontractors and trades people—Norman had decided, were not "professionals" like himself and the bankers.

As in all families, some members were more able to do the work than others; the various Tishmans possessed different mixes of abilities and personality characteristics. David was a tough guy, very sure of himself yet always willing to listen to what I had to say. He was a generation older and savvier than Norman, who tended to be more intractable and less sure of himself. Both of them had more on the ball than Alex, a judgment acknowledged by the succession, which skipped brother Alex and went directly to youngest brother Norman.

*Six Tishmans, 1963. I'm the second from the left.*
*The others, from left to right: my cousins Edward, Peter, Bob, and Alan,*
*and, seated center, our uncle, Norman.*

Everyone in the company and throughout the real estate industry knew that my cousin Bob Tishman was very sharp but also quite shy and introverted; his brother Alan, by contrast, was extroverted, a very nice guy with an outgoing personality. Alan's charm, which was considerable, was augmented by that of his wife, Peggy, a dynamic woman who became the leader of one of New York's largest charitable organizations. Alan was "Mr. Outside" to Bob's "Mr. Inside." Of the other cousins, Edward was engaging and eventually became a salesman, but he was not well suited for anything having to do with construction. His brother Bill, the closest cousin to me in age, was more interested in skiing and other athletic pursuits, and liked to socialize in Hollywood. It had taken him several more years to complete his engineering degree than it did me, which put him after me in the line of succession. Peter,

*One of the early buildings constructed by Tishman Real Estate,*
*935 Park Avenue, in 1923.*

Norman's only son, joined us later, was never far up in the hierarchy, and later went off and "did his own thing."

One fact that I did not learn about Tishman Realty until much later was what had happened to the firm during the Depression. Even though the firm had done okay right after the stock markets fell in October 1929, in the spring of 1931, as a company history put it, "Rental defaults built up swiftly, and arrears mounted into the millions within a matter of months. The firm's carefully accumulated reserves were wiped out within a short period of time, as operating costs remained constant and virtually all income ceased." Because of these problems, after my father's death David had gone to my mother with the assistance of an intermediary—a lawyer who had made out my father's will and was the trustee of his estate (in addition to being on the public Tishman company's board), a man whom my mother had been told she could trust with her life. Together, David and this lawyer prevailed upon her to sell back half of my father's stock, which Tishman Realty & Construction then resold to raise capital that they used to keep the company going. Many, many years later, when I found out about this hanky-panky wherein my uncles had taken money away from my mother, my brother, my sister and me, I was deeply shocked. By then there was nothing I could do about the situation, of course, having long since become ensconced in the company, but I never forgave Uncle David for using my mother's stock to help stave off the ravages of the Great Depression. He could well have preserved my mother's equity by pro-rating that stock across the stock owned by the families of all the other Tishman brothers.

## *The General Assistant and the "Tenements"*

My first assignment was as the assistant to our construction superintendent on two tenements that we were building in the Bronx, on Gun Hill Road. The word tenement gives some people the wrong impression. In New York City it's a technical term for a semi-fireproof, six-story, brick and wood building—not for a dilapidated ghetto residence. These two buildings were being erected under a financing program put in place by the Roosevelt Administration and administered by the Federal Housing Authority, the FHA. The man in charge of the company's construction, now that Paul had gone, was his former lieutenant, Joe Blitz. Blitz taught me a lot, but I also learned a great deal by observing and doing small tasks at the job site, not only by fetching coffee when that was wanted, but, more importantly, acting as the general assistant, file clerk, and timekeeper. One of the more telling tasks was to keep the daily log of which subcontractors and trades people came onto the job site, and what they did. It helped me learn the sequence of construction. As an engineer, I had some technical knowledge but no field experience. My degree and training probably affected how I observed and understood what was going on and going up.

The most significant revelation was of how the trades were interrelated, which demonstrated the importance of scheduling and coordination. Each trade was dependent, in sequence, on the others—for example, the bathroom pipes had to go in before the plumbers could install the toilets and sinks and bathtubs. Each trade had to show up and do its job, and coordinate with the others, as agreed to in the specs, or time would be lost and there would be claims by the later trades for interference. Speed of construction is very important for an owner-builder who has put money into a project and will be unable to recoup the investment (and pay off the construction loans) until the project is completed and rented out. For a general contractor, speed is less important, since his money is not similarly at risk during the project.

Blitz took me under his wing and brought me along as fast as he could. I didn't know it then, but he was planning to leave the company and join my uncle Paul in his general contracting business, which he soon did. Perhaps he wanted to get me up to some speed before he left the Tishman Realty firm.

During this period, the details of which are in the following few sections, I discovered that building and real estate were in my blood and that I was good at it. Because of the structure of the company, the lack of any other Tishman to take charge of the construction end, and the firm's own expansion in real estate development, my uncles provided me with plenty of opportunity to grow in the areas of design and construction management. The progression of ever-larger projects on which they embarked was far beyond the capacity of the few "construction people" left in the firm. As the only Tishman who seemed to be a "natural" at construction, this progression of projects made it possible for me to demonstrate my increasing competence and ascend to a responsible position on the design and construction side of the business. I liked the challenges, and, more particularly, the responsibilities that came my way. I started out liking the on-site supervision side of the jobs, and went on to take a shine to the creative pre-construction work in which I was able to participate as the voice of the owner, dealing with the architects and engineers during the development of the plans and specifications for each project. These projects afforded me various ways to develop and employ my creative juices during all the stages of creating apartment and office buildings. Looking back on this period, I know that I was very fortunate to have so many opportunities to "learn by doing" in so many different phases of the aesthetic and practical design process, as well as in the execution of very substantial construction projects in many areas of the country, and to do these projects as part of an ownership firm, rather than for outside owners.

## Doing the Strip Mall

Our next, and much larger project was in Queens, an 800-apartment complex on Woodlawn Avenue near the main thoroughfare of the borough, Queens Boulevard. The complex included a small strip mall. By this time, Joe Blitz had gone over to Paul's shop and David and Norman had hired a man to replace him. They thought this replacement guy was terrific because he had a book in which he proudly displayed his construction licenses from 48 states. David and Norman presumed that he had supervised construction in all those states, but I didn't buy that logic; I guessed that the reason this man had so many licenses was that he hadn't been hired a second time in any one state—a sure sign of only marginal competence. Eventually I came to believe that he had obtained some of the licenses at a distance, taking exams by mail. How did I figure this out? Well, he wasn't very good. He'd given out a subcontract based on an estimate that even I, a relative neophyte, thought was wrong, and he had then been surprised when the job wasn't brought in on time or on budget. His so-so competence actually provided me with another opportunity, as it was a void that my uncles could recognize and that I could fill. I was given sole charge of a portion of the complex, a small strip mall section adjacent to the FHA complex.

As construction tasks go, this was a very small one, but as with all such tasks it had to be done correctly and efficiently. I recognized this as a significant challenge, and responded. It was certainly an opportunity for me to learn by doing, and to go beyond being an observer. Now I was an overseer, and people listened to me, in part because I was a Tishman, an owner and not just a hired assistant.

I liked the job more when I had greater responsibilities, and that's what the strip mall job did for me; I helped with the design, awarded contracts, supervised the construction, processed permits, etc. Though small, the job entailed every trade: carpentry, plumbing, electrical, roofing, excavation, foundations, and the like. I took to going to the site on weekends just to see it when it wasn't busy. This was helpful, among other reasons because my presence there on weekends enabled me to see a few things going awry.

Contractors, whether a general contractor or subcontractors, submit bids, have them accepted by the owner and partially paid for, and then must deliver the work for the amount of money in the bid. This arrangement means that they always have an incentive to shave here and there, to cut corners, to raise their profits—or, if they had underbid the job, to prevent their losing money on the job.

One subcontractor at the strip mall, an excavator and foundation man, tried to save money by not properly dealing with a huge boulder dug up on the site. The correct procedure was to break it up into pieces and cart it away. This guy buried it right in the midst of the structure to be. Had I kept to a regular, weekdays-only schedule, we might not have known that the boulder had been buried until too late, when the structure had been erected over the burial site, which would have made removal of the boulder almost impossible and surely very expensive. But I found the burial site on one of my weekend visits, and we then revised the structural framing to be supported around the boulder.

The finding presented a good lesson for me, namely that someone representing the owner should be present at a construction site at night and on the weekends. Those are the times when the people who have the equipment to move boulders, or to deliver very large items to a construction site, will have the opportunity (and the equipment and the personnel) with which to reverse the burial activity or to abscond with the items they had previously delivered to the project.

A second problem that I caught by being at the site on a Saturday was a serious case of pilfering. In general, construction people know to lock up their valuable materials at night and on the weekends, because such materials will otherwise be stolen. Locking up such materials was routinely done at this site, with the exception of coaxial cable. It was very expensive, hard to obtain, and for some reason could be delivered only on Fridays. However on Saturdays, unbeknownst to us, someone would back up a truck and the cable would disappear for resale else-where. The cable and the copper pipes were very valuable and easily resold. For weeks, the electrician and plumbing foremen complained that their cable and copper pipe were being stolen and we'd tried to figure out by whom. But during those weeks none of us had been pres-ent on a Saturday. When I made my first Saturday visit, I caught the scam in progress. The people responsible, the electrical foreman and several plumbers, were fired, and we got back to work with some new faces on site.

My performance at the strip mall convinced Uncle David, who was still in charge, that I could be trusted not only to perform competently but also to view things from an owner's perspective—to mind the money on the construction site as though it was my own.

## Uncle Alex's Little Black Book

On the next project, with the book-of-licenses guy on the way out, I was confronted with a book of another kind.

The project was called Sutton Terrace, and it was to be an all-concrete, high-rise apartment building in Manhattan, on York Avenue between 62nd and 63rd Streets. In contrast to my previous two projects, this was designed as a two-building luxury complex with a garden on top of a multistoried underground garage. On this project I became the assistant to an old-time construction superintendent. The site, being within walking distance of the Tishman offices, was very visible to the family. Uncle Alex visited there frequently, and was generally accompanied by his son Bill, who came into the company during the construction of Sutton Terrace.

Bill was just starting in the company. He was an engineer with a degree that it had taken him quite a long time to obtain, and he did not seem terribly interested in construction nor, for that matter, in learning. He was becoming a champion skier and led a fabulous social life. But in the company's terms he had one thing that I didn't have—a patron, his father, Alex. Within the Tishman hierarchy, my uncles thought but never stated overtly, Bill and I were to be competitors.

Bill and Alex would visit Sutton Terrace while it was under construction. They'd talk to various foremen and such—almost never to me—and then jot down their notes in a little black notebook, notes

*99 Park Avenue. Its all-aluminum façade was erected in just six days.*

that were almost always about things that were supposedly being done wrong, things they thought that I was responsible for. Their black book was a report card on me to be shown to Uncle David, a way of documenting where I was falling short, so that Bill could be advanced over me.

When Sutton Terrace was finished, I rented a ground-floor apartment in the north building, an apartment that had a separate ground-floor entrance from the street and had been intended as a doctor's office. Prior to that, I had lived in my mother's apartment. Shortly, after my marriage, "my" apartment was re-rented to a psychiatrist, and my wife and I bought an apartment in a building that the company was converting into a co-op, uptown on Park Avenue.

I had met Susan Weisberg of Cleveland, and we had decided to marry in 1951. That was going to add to my responsibilities but I was ready for it. I was perhaps more ready for Tishman's next construction project, although it was a step up so large that I don't think my uncles would have allowed me to do it if they'd had anyone else available. An FHA-financed contractor had run into difficulties erecting a 2,000-unit complex called Ivy Hill, near South Orange, New Jersey, and had asked Tishman to take over the job, for a fee.

Construction for a fee was something the Tishman firm had never done before, but it was logical and the opportunity was available, and my uncles decided to accept it. There were to be four towers, cookie-cutter sort of buildings, each with 520 apartments, and twenty stories tall. This was a huge construction job, and I helped to put together a team to supervise the work. As a young man with only a modest amount of experience, I should have been a little more sobered than I was by the size of the project—but I wasn't. Bigger just meant more details to keep in my head and manage; and after all, I had taken to the management side of construction supervision like a duck to water.

At Ivy Hill, I was pretty much on my own. The guy with the book of licenses was completely gone by then. Cousin Bob was in nominal charge of construction, but he had no interest in the bricks and mortar, so he handled most of the business relationships with the project owners and interfaced with the banks and the FHA supervisors, while trusting me to do what was needed in respect to the various contractors involved, supervising and approving all matters of quality, cost, monthly payments to the subcontractors, and other job-site matters.

*Sue, our children, and me in Central Park, 1965.*

Alex and Bill were still in construction, but they didn't come to the site very often, since it was not within easy commuting distance of the Manhattan headquarters.

But they did show up occasionally and tramp around. Uncle Alex, with his muddy feet, looked like a bricklayer or laborer. He also seemed uncomfortable on site, and he always carried his little black book in which he would record his surmises about what was going wrong with the project. His notes had to do with such things as particular tradesmen not showing up for work, or tradesmen putting in too few hours on the job, a little delay here, a minor supply glitch there. Why was the concrete being poured so far ahead of the mechanicals? Why had some toilets been lost? Were the bricklayers really behind because of inadequate performance by the other trades?

Next day, at company headquarters, David would call me into his office, show me the notes from the black book, and ask about these "problems," for instance, the tradesman not putting in a full day.

"So what?" I would answer, more calmly than I felt. I contended that the problem was minor, inconsequential; it was the subcontractor's responsibility, I argued, to see that his people showed up every day and put in the requisite amount of time. Since we were paying the subcontractor a previously negotiated flat price, if he couldn't get his own people to do the work he would be the loser, not us. David and I would go down the list of "problems" and talk back and forth about the notations in the black notebook. None of the small difficulties was holding us up in any significant way or was cause for alarm on the part of higher management, I argued. All were matters that I could deal with by myself, and had been dealing with on a regular basis, without bothering David. Eventually I had to contend to David that Alex and Bill had simply brought these minor matters to his attention to show me up, as a cover for their noninvolvement and to boost Bill's greater involvement in construction in the hope that he could replace me.

David did not disagree with my analysis.

Looking back on it, I think that David asked me the questions from the little black book so he could then inform Alex that he had done so, and also tell Alex that I had been doing a fine job. Whatever, I remained in charge of the project at Ivy Hill and successfully saw it through to completion. And in doing so I effectively leaped over my cousins in the construction area and became the de facto supervisor of construction for Tishman Realty & Construction. Shortly, Bill was sent to Los Angeles to be an assistant supervisor on a construction project in California. He developed into a Hollywood character, frequenting nightclubs and perfecting his skiing. Not too long after becoming established in Hollywood, he left Tishman Realty of his own volition.

## *In Charge?*

The next building Tishman was going to erect, for its own real estate portfolio, was just below Grand Central Station, 99 Park Avenue, a twenty-six-story office building. This was not a project in the outlying boroughs or the suburbs; rather, it was one that all of our competitors (and prospective tenants) would be able to see as it went up. And I was going to be in full charge of its construction. It was about three years since I'd joined the company, and I looked forward to being in charge. I had come to like construction, liked the rough and tumble of it, especially dealing with the construction workers who were generally hardworking and very good at what they did and who enjoyed being carpenters, plumbers, and cement workers. I liked getting information from subcontractors and then negotiating with them, and being out on the site. What I liked most was having a substantial part in practical and creative aspects of the architectural, structural, and mechanical designs, and not having anyone in the family second-guessing me. Alex was still involved in construction, but by this point he knew not to challenge what I was doing in the planning—or to show up on the job site with his little black book.

Tishman Realty & Construction had a history of putting up somewhat innovative buildings, going back to the 1920s, and 99 Park was going to be a showcase. It was going to be one of the first buildings in which there were only to be self-service elevators, and that presented some design challenges. We immediately realized that the elevator cabs, since there would be no operator present, would be vulnerable to vandalism and graffiti. I helped to come up with an answer to that problem. Another design challenge was the façade. I had been working with Alcoa, and we had come up with a way to use their aluminum for the façade instead of bricks or stone and mortar. To put on bricks and mortar was a process that often took weeks. Alcoa's aluminum façade for 99 Park, a building of twenty-seven stories, with the aluminum wrapping around three sides, was going to be installed in just five days. (I'll detail these innovations, and others, in the next chapter.)

Saving money on construction while being innovative enough to provide the company with a good public relations opportunity was reason enough for my uncles to celebrate me, but although they were appreciative of me and enjoyed the corporate kudos they received for our construction work, I was still considered the family outsider.

How much of an outsider was brought home to me when one of my construction department draftsmen showed me a chart commissioned by David Tishman that I wasn't supposed to see. He had been asked by Uncle David to draw it up and not to tell anyone. "I shouldn't show this to you," the man said, but added that since he reported directly to me, he felt I should see it.

It was a succession chart of Tishman family members, showing how the company was expected to evolve over time. Henceforth, with David still as chairman, there would be three distinct divisions: development, leasing, and construction. Norman was to head up the company and particularly real estate development, and my cousin, Bob, would eventually succeed him in those slots. Cousin Alan would head the management and leasing division, aided by various other cousins. All of my cousins were on the chart. I was not. The draftsman asked me whether I was planning to retire or whether I thought they had just forgotten me.

This chart shocked me. In David's vision of the company's future, I had no role. However, I didn't immediately charge into his office and confront him about it although I was quite upset. Perhaps I didn't confront him with it because I didn't want to have the needed argument when I was that upset. Some time later, though, I found the opportunity to confront him about the chart.

"Why am I not on it?"

"That chart doesn't mean anything," he said, arguing that it had been just an exercise for the purpose of gaming things out. "Oh, it's just like you, worrying," he continued. "You'll have a place. You may even be in charge of construction ... someday."

My uncle didn't realize, or didn't want to acknowledge, that the entire non-family staff of our company, and all the tradespeople we dealt with, already thought I was in charge of construction.

# *Innovations*

## *Expanding Company Horizons and Mine, Too*

In 1950, when I was still relatively new at Tishman Realty, the company was expanding its operations beyond New York City. We were completing what was called the mid-Wilshire project in Los Angeles, three moderate-sized buildings at 3440, 3350, and 3360 Wilshire Boulevard. In creating these, Tishman Realty was continuing to pursue the sort of projects that had served it well in New York City—pioneering in terms of the area in which we built as well as in terms of the type of buildings we would erect there, in this instance, office buildings where before there had mainly been small storefronts and residences. The mid-Wilshire buildings were Uncle Norman's projects; Uncle David was not keen on them because we had had to hire a local architect and a local general contractor, making for a situation in which, in his view, we lost some control of the project's architecture and construction. Furthermore, construction in Los Angeles presented additional problems for us as developers; because of earthquake probabilities, the building codes would not permit the erecting of a building taller than twelve stories, a small size that limited the potential profitability of an office building. The code was outmoded in this regard, because in recent

*Century City in Los Angeles, built for Alcoa, and designed by
Yamasaki, its façade an echo of his World Trade Center.*

years construction materials and techniques had improved, but the
code had not been changed.

Perhaps it was because there were so many problems and potential downsides, rather than upsides, that when the third mid-Wilshire
building was ready to be constructed, and I had gained my uncles' confidence as a construction supervisor, I was put in charge of building
it. During that project, and for years thereafter on others in the area, I
would fly to California on a regular basis—a time-consuming matter in
the era before there were jet, non-stop, coast-to-coast flights.

The sites in California were pioneering for Los Angeles, and for our
firm, but as far as construction went, these first L.A. projects were
pretty standard stuff. However, in some projects closer to home I found
many opportunities to also pioneer various aspects of construction.

I might not have realized this at the time, but today, after a lifetime of making such innovations, I have become convinced that successful design and construction innovations could have been effectively conceived and tried out only by an "owner/builder." A general contractor cannot afford to make or even to suggest radical innovations because his job is simply to execute from existing plans and not to deviate from them; neither can an owner/developer whose company does not closely and personally oversee the actual job site construction. Only those deeply involved in the design and construction aspects of the project, and who have the benefit—and the needs—of being the owner/builder, or acting on behalf of an owner/builder, can do so. The Tishman Company as owner/builders could accept the risk of experimenting with new processes and materials—because we were in a position to bear the costs if something went wrong and to reap the benefits if the new methods or materials worked well. Becoming better-versed in construction and in controlling costs, I was able to see and take advantage of opportunities in which innovation was likely to pay off for our firm.

Innovating became one of the most satisfying aspects of my work. I don't think I would have enjoyed my career as much if it had simply consisted of executing construction from plans solely developed by others. By dreaming up innovations on our own projects, and, later, by suggesting for projects done for other owners not only new devices and materials but also new methodologies of construction, I was able to maintain my interest and make each new project an interesting challenge. My most important innovation would be the concept of Construction Management; the idea for this evolved over a period of years, and, accordingly, later chapters in this book will trace its development and importance.

The idea of Construction Management lay in the far future when my opportunities to innovate began, with the construction in 1953 of 99 Park Avenue, the office tower just south of Grand Central Station. This building project birthed several specific technical innovations as well as the chartering of the Tishman Research Corporation, which partnered with various industrial manufacturers and trade subcontractors to do research on materials and systems—a division of Tishman Realty that became my pet.

I had a history of tinkering. For years, wherever I'd lived, I had my own woodworking shop, and had always been interested in creating things in them. Tishman Realty provided me with opportunities to marshal this interest for the benefit of the project, the company, and—with the cooperation of the materials manufacturers and the trade subcontractors—for the entire construction field.

Tishman Realty prided itself on "value engineering," the adding of value to a design element by making it better in some way—longer lasting, easier to install, less costly to install, maintain and/or operate, or otherwise enhancing its functions. To be really useful, any such innovation must perform in ways that integrate smoothly with the efforts of those who actually build and manage the finished project; that utility goal is more readily achieved when the innovations are done for a company, such as ours, involved in every aspect of the project from development and financing through construction and on to leasing the space.

Through Tishman Research Corporation, we were able to induce materials manufacturers to become more innovative by holding out the certainty that if the new product was good enough, Tishman Realty would buy and use it in a real-life, million-square-foot office building. Knowing that the product could be sold in quantity was enough of an enticement for a materials company to make the costly decision to refit a production line so that it could turn out new configurations of flooring or ceiling modules or of exterior panels. Without such a promise of sales in the offing, a manufacturer would be reluctant to invest in revamping its tools and procedures to manufacture a new or radically improved product.

Our substantial office building being constructed at 99 Park Avenue in Manhattan was an ideal laboratory in which to innovate in methods and materials, among other reasons because it was to be a multi-tenanted office building that our company would lease out and maintain. Apartment houses afforded fewer opportunities for invention because apartments tended to be standardized units, and fairly small in terms of floor space when compared to offices. Then, too, the fact that we would be managing the building encouraged innovations that would cut down not only on initial costs but on later, continuing expenditures—an advantage that could accrue to our benefit and to that of our commercial tenants.

## *Light from the Ceilings*

Developers of office buildings in that era would provide prospective tenants with certain "building standard improvements," typically the floor covering, ceiling system, and light fixtures. We would guarantee an illumination level of a certain number of watts per square foot, and then go about spacing the lighting fixtures to provide that level. We would also offer several variations of such configurations for a single price.

Innovative interiors and tenant installations were a selling point for our firm's office buildings. One such innovation involved changing the module for office space ceiling tiles. Prior to this time the standard ceiling tile modular size was 1x1 foot, but the standard for fluorescent lighting fixtures was 1x4 feet. That meant four fluorescent lamps had to be squeezed into a one-foot wide metal shell, and this crowding created so much heat that the bulbs were literally fried and their efficiency and life expectancy dramatically reduced. The crowded space was also a magnet for dust and all sorts of insects attracted by the bright lights. This made for high operating costs, since the bulbs had to be replaced frequently and the fixtures cleaned often to produce the expected light levels.

The logical solution, it seemed to me, was to increase the space between the bulbs so that the heat they put out was more easily dissipated, allowing the bulbs to last substantially longer. My former math student Fred Shure joined me in trying to solve the problem.

We increased the size of the ceiling tiles that had been traditionally 1x4 foot, to 2x4 feet. This simple change allowed the four fluorescent light bulbs to be spread apart within a 24-inch-wide fixture, instead of within the smaller space that had been the previous standard throughout the industry. In this way the fluorescent bulbs were no longer fried by the others' proximity, and there was no decrease in the light available at desk height. We worked with the manufacturers to fabricate these larger ceiling panels and light fixtures, and installed them as the "tenant standard" throughout the 99 Park Avenue building. Not only did the fixtures allow the bulbs to last much longer, but because the acoustic panels and lighting fixtures were wider and removable, the spaces above the hung ceiling were easier to get at for cleaning and alterations. Additionally, the quality of light at desktop height was far superior to the older configuration, since it was spread more evenly.

The 2x4 fluorescents then became the standard throughout the industry, and the ceiling module became pretty much the standard throughout the country. Neither Fred nor I was able to make any money from this innovation because it was so easily copied, but we had the satisfaction of having created a nationwide standard. Fred went on to my alma mater, Michigan, for his undergraduate work and then to Harvard, where he earned a Ph.D. in physics. I was energized by this innovation, and went looking for other nationwide standards that we could upgrade.

## *Beating Graffiti, Panel by Panel*

The Tishman firm had been pioneers in the use of central air-conditioning, fluorescent lighting, and automatic elevators. The 99 Park building was going to be one of the first office towers to have only self-service elevators. That was a plus for us in terms of being able to rent the building, but it also presented a few problems that would not have been obvious to anyone other than a company whose business included managing buildings as well as developing and constructing them.

The one benefit of having human operators in elevators during the business day was that their presence prevented the elevator cabs from being vandalized by people who scratched graffiti on the elevator panels, and otherwise besmirched the cabs. Because such elevators had always had operators in them, discouraging damage to the cabs, not much thought had been given to ease of repair or of replacement of cab interiors. Perhaps this was why early elevator panels had been designed in such a way that they could be accessed for replacement or repair only when the cab was out of service. Even then, working on the panels was a laborious process. You could remove the wall panels only from the outside, by first unscrewing the exterior fasteners, then lifting out the heavy panels, etc. The difficulty of servicing the panels was why the vandalized panels of some self-service cabs had been let go to the point that they could no longer be cleaned and had to be replaced. Building managers knew that graffiti-type vandalism, once it started, only became worse: a second would-be "writer," recognizing that someone had previously marked up or scratched graffiti on the elevator cab, would have fewer compunctions about adding to the damage. But because taking off the panels was so laborious, these initial graffiti were often ignored, with disastrous results.

I worked with the leading elevator cab manufacturer to design panels that could be mounted inside of the elevator with specially designed fasteners (rather than bolted on from outside), the panels then could be easily removed and cleaned or replaced without having to take the cab apart. I developed a hanging mechanism that connected the panels to the cab in such a way that it became easy to clean them regularly, should graffiti "art" be written on them, or to easily remove and exchange them for newer ones if the damage was too severe to be repaired.

I was able to patent this very simple hanging device, and for many years thereafter received modest royalties on it. But that had not been my objective; rather, the point had been to design something that would save us, as building owners, on our operating costs. It also served to keep the elevators looking much newer and cleaner, an important selling point for tenants.

## An Aluminum Façade

The most spectacular innovation on 99 Park Avenue had to do with the façade. The exterior was to be made of aluminum panels that would not only be weather-resistant but could be installed quickly after the superstructure had been advanced to the point of being ready to support it. The usual way of putting on a façade was slow and laborious, with bricks and mortar laid painstakingly by hand, floor after floor. That process of completing the façade could take weeks, and in the sort of commercial office building construction that Tishman Realty did, speed of construction was of the essence. Market conditions could change, and too much lead time between when a building was conceived and when it was ready for occupancy could compromise the building's profitability if rents declined in the interim. A façade that could be erected in a matter of days rather than weeks was a big help. At 99 Park, it took just six-and-a-half days to install the façade on all three exposed sides of the building. Also, being made of aluminum, this façade took up less space on the building's exterior than one made of bricks and mortar would have done. The aluminum was also a lot less expensive to install because scaffolding did not have to be constructed or moved—ropes and men inside the building could maneuver the two-floor-high panels into the right locations and bolt them into place. Each panel contained two windows and two spandrel panels, stacked vertically, as well as an aluminum frame to hold the whole thing together. Adjacent aluminum panels dovetailed into one another, eliminating the need for caulking. This saved money in two ways, in the cost of installation and in terms of lower maintenance costs. Fixing leaks is always costly and, if the leaks are coming from the façade rather than from the roof, they are rather difficult to remedy.

I am proud that for more than fifty years the entire aluminum-cladding system at 99 Park has remained watertight, therefore requiring no maintenance, caulking or other significant remedial work.

On the next building we constructed for ourselves, 460 Park Avenue at 57th Street, our research work with Alcoa and our expertise

*With the architects, looking over the plans for constructing our second headquarters, 460 Park Avenue.*

in attaching aluminum facades had advanced to the point where we figured that we would be able to hang the aluminum façade in a matter of hours rather than days. This, we also thought, was enough of an astonishing feat that it could get us some publicity. *Life* magazine agreed, and in early October 1960 they sent a photographer to document our installing all of the facades facing both Park Avenue and 57th Street in a single day. We even did better, completing the task in a mere thirteen hours—a hectic day but a great one. After it, we were expecting what *Life* had more or less promised, a centerfold story in the nation's leading pictorial magazine—when Soviet premier Nikita Khrushchev decided to bang his shoe on a desk at the United Nations to protest something said by another country's delegate, and *Life* decided that the shoe-banging was more newsworthy than our construction exploit, and relegated us to only an inside-the-magazine story. That aside, we did get quite a bit of positive press for the accomplishment. It even spawned interesting letters to me from people in Japan and in other foreign countries, inquiring if we could teach them how to erect an entire building in a single day.

Our very next building, again in Manhattan, was to be our expanded headquarters, 666 Fifth Avenue, and we decided that it, too, would have an aluminum façade. Alcoa's competitor, Reynolds Aluminum, of Reynolds Wrap fame, wanted in on the new field of building facades. Their top executives had wined and dined Uncle Norman and convinced him that we should have a version of the famous Reynolds Wrap on our headquarters. I wasn't so sure, since they had not done any research and did not have the experience that Alcoa did, but Uncle Norman made the decision, and at that time I did not feel that I could gainsay it. Although we had some severe problems all through the design and execution process, we and Reynolds eventually persevered. The building opened for business in January 1957, and to celebrate the creation of our greatly expanded headquarters, our stock was officially moved from the American Exchange to the larger New York Stock Exchange, an acknowledgement that Tishman Realty had become, as owner/builders, one of the country's leaders in high-rise construction.

After this episode with the façade of 666 Fifth, however, Reynolds decided not to pursue a product line of building wraps but continued their supremacy in food wraps.


## Tishman Research Corporation

Our wholly owned subsidiary Tishman Research Corporation became the vehicle for Tishman Realty's continuing innovations in architectural products and building systems. Having a subsidiary devoted to research and innovation was not something that other developers were willing to copy. One of those competitors later commented to a construction industry publication, "Let Tishman ... be the guinea pigs

*The Tishman Building, 666 Fifth Avenue, with its distinctive aluminum façade.*

and pay the cost of research and development. We'll hang back until the price comes down." And—they did not add, but I understood— until the product proved itself.

Joe Newman had come on board to head our research efforts, which I treasured and helped introduce to the architectural community and their clients. Interest in innovations within the industry picked up after 1962, when the initial postwar boom slowed and developers and manufacturers looked for ways to save money and/or provide better products and services for their clients. In 1976, President Gerald Ford appointed Newman as chief of the new federal agency, the National Institute of Building Sciences.

Among the most interesting projects of Tishman Research came during that period, an evaluation of a thousand tall office buildings, mostly federal buildings, throughout the country, done for the Public Buildings Service, a division of the General Services Administration. This time and costs analysis revealed—not surprising to us—that buildings put up using a Construction Management approach cost less and were much quicker to erect than those that had used the old methodology of completing a set of plans and putting them out to bid by a set of general contractors. (More about this in a later chapter about Construction Management.)

A second study of a thousand buildings in New York City, completed for the U.S. Department of Energy in 1978, revealed many inefficiencies in the design and use of energy sources. The study led directly to revised codes and controls for conserving energy in new buildings, and to ways to refit older buildings to curb energy waste.

## Projects in Many Places

Most of the New York owner/builders, in the late 1950s and early 1960s, followed a pattern in which they accumulated property over a period of years and then developed it. Tishman Realty tended to follow a different pattern. We'd get involved in acquiring a piece of land only when it was clear that we could erect on it, in the near future, a building with a given purpose—office, residential, or shopping center. Brokers all over the country knew of our pattern and frequently brought us projects. As a result, in those years we had projects going up in several cities across the country. For me, this meant being continually on airplanes, trekking out to supervise the design and construction of office buildings and high-rise apartment buildings in cities from Philadelphia to Los Angeles. The most memorable of these projects were the numerous office and residential structures along Wilshire Boulevard in Los Angeles, the East Ohio Gas building in Cleveland, the office complex known as 10 Lafayette Square in Buffalo, and high-rises in St. Louis, San Francisco, and Philadelphia.

There were innovations associated with nearly every one of these projects.

The two Philadelphia buildings, called Center City, were right in the heart of downtown, one for an oil company headquarters, the other for a bank. For these significant buildings, we decided to use a process in which the exterior as well as the structure was made of exposed, cast-in-place concrete, rather than the exterior being clad with marble or with the then-popular "curtain wall" of glass. The exposed concrete gave the building an interesting appearance and great structural strength while it saved money and time in construction.

On an apartment complex in Pittsburgh, in the downtown, Three Rivers area known as Gateway Center, we innovated by using a new type of window. The new window consisted of an outer pane of glass and an inner one separated from it by several inches, and containing within that space aluminum Venetian blinds. Usually, in office buildings that have conventional blinds, the blinds become dusty and are also a pain in the neck to maintain. But when we placed the blinds between two panes of glass, they were able to shade the interior offices just as well as conventional blinds would have done, but were easier and less expensive to maintain.

New windows and similar new products were made available to

all developers, but frequently we were the first developer to use them. We were never too timid to try something new because we were generally the owner as well as the builder, which allowed us the opportunity to either reap the benefits of such innovations in the construction or ownership phases, or suffer the consequences, should our pioneering produce bad results.

On an additional project in Los Angeles, we also pushed the envelope of what a developer could do. We erected the first new apartment building in all of California that was to be sold to tenants as a co-op. Early on, we sold some apartments to high-profile tenants whose presence then aided the sale of the other units. The most important of these high-profile owners was John Hertz, the founder of the Hertz car rental agency, who took half of the penthouse floor and had us put in a below-grade swimming pool just for him. Famed film director Mervyn LeRoy was another early buyer.

I remember one very embarrassing moment during a meeting with prospective tenant/buyers prior to the completion of the building: We were sitting in an interior space facing the garden, and our sales manager was extolling the high quality of the building when suddenly sheets of water came down outside the window. A plumber had disconnected a water line on the roof three floors above us, causing a flood. I quickly recovered by saying that we had designed a waterfall through which one could view the beautiful garden below. I got a couple of snickers, but perhaps my quick reaction helped, because the accident did not seem to have any negative impact on sales. Wilshire Terrace with its thirteen floors became the tallest building in Los Angeles at the time. After it, Los Angeles eliminated its height limitations for future buildings.

On the tops of all the office buildings we constructed and owned, we placed signs identifying them as Tishman properties, causing many locals to think of us as a California-based company.

## Cleveland, Buffalo, and the Glass Spandrels

My wife Susan Weisberg was born and brought up in Cleveland. A second cousin of hers came to see me in New York about a Cleveland site he knew was available for development, and a major bank that was looking to have a headquarters in the area. We made deals, first with my "cousin-in-law" for the property, and then with that bank to be the lead tenant in a building that we would erect.

After that building was well into construction, Superior Oil also wanted a building erected, across the street, that would serve as its headquarters, and we built that for them as well. The name of their subsidiary, for which the building was ultimately named, was the East Ohio Gas Company.

In a similar manner, the Niagara Electric Company, based in Buffalo, came to us requesting to be the major tenant in a building we were planning for a site we had acquired at 10 Lafayette Square in that city.

For the Cleveland building, and then for the Buffalo building, we designed the same kind of façades and contracted for the glass on both buildings to be fabricated and installed by Libby-Owens-Ford. LOF provided glass for Ford car windshields, and the glass to be used in these buildings would have properties similar to those required in auto windshields—it would be "tempered," so it wouldn't shatter if hit or compromised.

It was the era during which glass façades had become popular, after the creation of the first one, for the Lever House on Park Avenue in New York City. The façade was called a glass curtain wall, and it consisted of two parts. The lower part, called spandrel glass, was dark and non-transparent, and was tempered to withstand the tremendous heat that would build up from the midday sun and not dissipate, since no air would circulate behind the glass. The spandrel would cover the lower parts of the window wall, behind which were hidden the peripheral air-conditioning and heating units, as well as the building's structural elements. The second part of the façade was known as the "vision light," a light blue-green window glass that could be seen through from outside as well as from inside.

Construction of the curtain wall on the building in Cleveland was complete and that on the Buffalo building was partially completed when spiderweb cracks began to appear in the spandrel glass in both buildings, near the edges and always in the corners. This happened on about 15 percent of the spandrels in both buildings.

We were mystified as to why this had occurred, and so was LOF, the manufacturer of the glass. First, LOF tried to blame the cracks on birds flying head-on into the windows. How, I asked, could birds fly into the Cleveland and Buffalo buildings at around the same time? And why were there no bird carcasses on the streets below? When their explanations didn't carry the day, LOF began to blame us—it must be the fault of poor installation techniques. I refused to accept that explanation (or the responsibility for replacing the panels that it would have brought). We hired experts from MIT to look into the matter, and with the help of Tishman Research and of LOF's own research team, the researchers eventually found the culprits.

Yes, there was more than one culprit.

The immediate culprit was alternating blasts of hot and cold air on days that were broiling during the sun-filled hours yet were very cool, almost frigid, at night. But the original cause was—the tongs used during the tempering process. In that process, tongs were used to lift a panel out of one treatment procedure and convey it into another. Research discovered that the cracks in the glass began at the tiny points where the tongs had made impressions on the panels as they were used to lift and carry the glass panels from one bath to another. These minute impressions on the tempered glass, over a period of time, would cause the panels to crack.

The compromised panels were replaced, the production process for the tempered glass was changed so that the tongs would not dig into the glass, and the new panels on both buildings were tested for problems—in place—by an ingenious process of heating and forced-cooling conducted from outside the building on hanging scaffolds. After an extraordinary effort and considerable time, construction on both projects was completed. Since then, so far as I know, the curtain walls have held up—a matter of almost fifty years. And so—one hopes—thus ends the tale of two cities.

## Russians on the Roof

One of our Tishman Research projects, conducted jointly with a leading roofing-materials manufacturer, had to do with an experimental roofing compound just developed by that manufacturer. This innovation would hardly be of interest except for the brouhaha it created that had to do with the Russians in Riverdale. The Soviet Union's bigwigs had decided to construct a new facility to house their people who served the U.N. as well as at their counsel in New York, to be built on the highest point of land in the Riverdale section of the Bronx. They also planned to use a construction method invented by a Russian engineer but untried in the U.S. They approached us to be the Construction Manager of the job; our relationship was somewhat complicated, as it was entirely dependent upon an intermediary who had obtained the contract for us and to whom the Soviets would send money for through-payment to us. Since the Russian government had purchased the land, their ownership conveyed to the land diplomatic immunity from New York's complex building codes. Even so, the Soviets were interested in adhering to all our building codes; however, this presented substantial difficulties because some of their building techniques and installation requirements were not easily accepted by our trade unions, particularly in terms of which union was to perform what installation.

The FBI found out about our contract with the Soviets and came to see me in my office at 666 Fifth Avenue. Men with sober suits, white ties, and serious faces wanted access to the building site during the construction period. They didn't say what for, but it was obvious to me that their purpose was to place hidden microphones and other such espionage devices. This was during the height of the Cold War and my patriotic duty was clear. I offered to call Abe Levine, our project executive for the assignment, and tell him that they wanted to speak with him. However they insisted that they needed to check out Abe's background before they would speak to him; they asked where Abe lived, and I told them it was in Brooklyn or Queens. I reached for the phone to ask our payroll department for Abe's home address. They stopped me in my tracks and told me that they would prefer to locate Abe themselves. A month or so later, the two FBI fellows returned and, embarrassed, asked me whether I knew how many Abe Levines lived in Brooklyn and Queens. Unable to locate Abe themselves, this time they allowed me to obtain his address for them. The very next day, Abe let me know that the FBI had visited him. I suppose the FBI went ahead and installed listening devices but I never knew for sure.

In any event, I suggested to our clients, the Russians, that on this project we try a new mastic roofing material that we had under research, and they agreed. Unfortunately, this experimental material didn't work out very well. On the first very hot summer day, it cracked, and thereafter it leaked. I offered to have the roof fixed or replaced, but the Russians said no. The reason was clear: they didn't want anyone from our company or any other U.S. citizens on their premises, particularly on the roof, now that the building had become operational, so they determined to fix the roof leaks themselves. They actually brought over eight laborers from the USSR, had them buy smearing materials at local hardware stores in the Bronx, and proceeded to repair the roof.

Near the end of our contract, the intermediary between us and the Soviets went bankrupt, and we never obtained our last payment.

*A topping-off ceremony for the Russian consulate in the Riverdale section of the Bronx.*

Seeing no alternative, we were resigned to write it off; however, one of our subcontractors, who also hadn't received his payment, was not. He had gone to considerable expense to manufacture an unusually wide door for the garage. After his many attempts to obtain payment for the work had failed, this subcontractor decided to take another route. He and his workmen showed up at this ultra-secret Soviet facility in the middle of the night; they brought their truck right up to the building, removed the special door they had made, and carted it back to their factory. How had they gotten past the security detail? I don't know, but my guess is that the night watchman at the Soviet compound must have been an FBI operative who saw fit to cooperate with the subcontractor's nighttime repo raid.

## *Concrete Dust*

Speaking of people ripping things off in the night brings me to the Mob. Construction is known as a rough business, and popular fiction always has it "controlled" by the Mob. Actually, in my life in construction, which covers nearly six decades, I encountered very little of that. My most interesting brush with it involved a concrete contractor.

The story is a bit complicated. We were building a post office in Manhattan, one that needed a lot of concrete. We were also building a series of apartment towers on the Palisades in New Jersey. Generally, we use only New York firms for concrete construction, but in this instance, since we needed a lot of concrete work in both areas, we decided on a New Jersey concrete firm.

There were some minor glitches, and we had a small dispute about the concrete for the Manhattan post office. Usually, with such disputes, we are able to resolve them readily through payments from one party to the other. However, in this instance, the New Jersey firm was reluctant to settle with us, and we took them to court and won. After that, the head man insisted that I meet him on the job site in the Palisades.

At the appointed hour in the mid-afternoon, I showed up on the Palisades site, and waited. Some time later a large white Cadillac entered the site and sped toward me, kicking up a huge cloud of dust as it did. The Caddy came to a halt not far from me but the dust continued to roll over me, in choking proportions. I coughed and coughed. And felt menaced, a feeling that did not resolve when the big guy got out of his car, with a bulge under his jacket indicating he was "packing heat."

Nonetheless, I proceeded to negotiate with this gentleman from New Jersey as though I wasn't scared, and we did come to an arrangement that did not leave me feeling ripped off. I went back home and, needless to say, we never again employed that firm in our construction endeavors.

## *From Wet to Dry*

For many generations, stairwells and elevator shafts had been the prov-ince of what construction people called the "wet trades." These areas were constructed using gypsum blocks or wire lath that were smeared with a heavy coat of fire retardant vermiculite, or with exposed cinder blocks that were painted or, less frequently, left bare. Such fire-resistant walls worked well enough for a long time, but in the 1950s we began to look for alternatives because block construction was labor-intensive to install and required the use of temporary heat when being installed in cold weather.

There was a need for materials and systems that were the equal in fireproof or fire-resistant performance to the old cinder blocks and masonry. Tishman Research worked with the largest Sheetrock manu-facturer, U.S. Gypsum, to come up with a new wall design that would meet the requirements of New York City's Fire Department and Build-ings Department, and to make certain that the new walls would also be up to all the requirements for national codes. We also wanted to pass muster with the Underwriters Lab, an insurance-industry group. We did all of this with the product that we named Shaft Wall. Our first use of the Shaft Wall was in a building at 100 Gold Street in Manhattan, which we built for our own portfolio and in which the city's Buildings Department was to be a major tenant.

In later years, Tishman Research consulted to New York City's Department of Buildings on the renovation of fire and safety codes, contributing to what was known as Local Law Number 5, which other jurisdictions in the United States soon copied.

The drywall construction that we helped develop became the industry standard for elevator shaft walls. Consisting of multiple lay-ers of Sheetrock, these new walls were lighter in weight and easier and quicker to install. Also, they were naturally straight and smooth, and when they were installed in winter, did not require temporary heat. With the use of these new walls, whose plasterboard took up a smaller area than the old blocks had done, stairwells became more spacious.

Speaking of walls, when we built our flagship building, 666 Fifth Avenue, we innovated by installing movable flat metal panel partitions throughout the building—the first office building to use this sort of technology throughout its spaces as a "tenant standard." The panels enclosed soundproofing material inside. Relatively easy to install, the panels also made it possible to reconfigure space precisely to suit each new tenant. They also paid off in later years because they were so much easier to remove and to replace than the old interior lath and plaster walls had been, and the panels were generally reusable—if one tenant in a building didn't want them, the panels could be taken out and installed elsewhere, at very low cost to us.

## Ninety-seven Steps to Making a Bathroom?

Shaft walls and metal partitions were examples of prefabricated components that we developed and pioneered. Many other organizations were also developing prefab components, and I was always interested in them. The obvious reason for this interest is that they are easier and quicker to install; the less-obvious reason is that when components are manufactured and fitted together in a factory, there is greater quality control than there is when various parts are put together at a building site.

It was not always easy to employ prefab components on large construction projects because their installation often cuts across union jurisdictional lines, which can cause problems. However, our company was always in a good position to solve such problems because we regularly worked closely with the unions and became a well-known champion of using unionized workers on the job. I would tell anyone who listened—the media, other developers and construction people, even prospective tenants—that we actually saved money by using unionized labor because the unionized tradesmen were better trained, more experienced, and more productive.

Our reputation enabled us to head off some potential disputes regarding prefab products. Before construction began, I would call in the leaders of the two or three unions that I thought might have a jurisdictional fight over new prefabricated systems and components, and we'd settle in advance which of the trades would handle a particular type of panel or module—the carpenter, the plumber, the tile installer, the sheetmetal worker, or some combination of these. We'd work it out, and then construction could proceed without trade conflicts.

For the hemisphere's largest all-concrete hotel, at Detroit's Renaissance Center, for which we were serving as Construction Manager, we helped design completely pre-fabricated bathroom component systems. We were able to demonstrate to the materials producers that there were ninety-seven different steps in the construction of a bathroom, and that about a quarter of those steps could be eliminated. That entailed producing a bathroom system with only six basic pieces, most of which used new manufacturing techniques. For instance, by getting rid of the need to have two knobs on a tub, one for cold and one for hot, and substituting a one-piece control, lots of fabrication time to make the unit, as well as installation time, could be saved—and, as we all know, saving time means saving money. We also worked with a manufacturer to create a one-piece, wall-to-wall vanity that was easier to manufacture and install.

## Infracon

Innovation doesn't always have to entail inventing something yourself; sometimes, you innovate by making it possible to use another person's breakthrough that otherwise might have sat unused. That's what happened with us in regard to a device that we named Infracon.

During the 1973 Middle East War, the oil-producing nations embargoed the sale of oil from that region to the United States, making oil scarce and expensive to American consumers, and as a consequence, spurring research into energy conservation. Tishman Research worked with federal and state agencies, and industrial companies, to come up with new ways for buildings to conserve more energy. The cost of electricity, which had gone up as a consequence of rising oil prices, was a significant factor in the operating costs of all buildings, and we looked for ways to lower that. We worked jointly with United Technologies to cut electricity use. One obvious target was lights that were usually left on all night so that cleaning crews could work in office buildings. Was it necessary to have the lights on during all the night hours, a period when most employees were not working in their offices? Of course not. So if we could figure out a way to douse the lights whenever no one was in the office for a stretch of time, that would save money and also conserve energy.

Infrared sensors are able to detect the presence of small heat changes. We reasoned that a device that used an infrared sensor could be affected by very small temperature changes, and might be able to detect the sort of changes that are inevitably produced by human beings as they move within a room. We further reasoned that the absence of movement in a room for a given number of seconds or minutes would denote a lack of need for lights to be on in that room, and provide an opportunity for a relay to switch off the lights in that space. We purchased a sensor system that an inventor had not previously found a use for. We boxed it with relays to control high voltage and called it Infracon. United Technologies manufactured it for us. We installed the new heat-and-motion sensors in buildings that we built for ourselves, particularly in the conference and meeting rooms of our hotels, and in several instances, in areas within buildings that we built for others.

Beyond saving money in use of electricity, Infracon provided benefits in terms of building security. The sensors functioned as a back-up security system, able to signal to guards at the front desk when someone was in an office upstairs—someone other than an authorized cleaning crew; for example, a burglar. We ultimately sold our rights in Infracon to an electrical contractor who in turn resold it to Minneapolis Honeywell. I am delighted whenever I see Infracon technology incorporated into other devices in which even minor heat variations in the air are used to trigger protective action, particularly if this usage results, as it is supposed to, in saving energy.

# THREE

# *Building Tall*

## *The New Garden*

Madison Square Garden is an old name with a long history. The first building with that name had begun in 1871 as a new appellation for an older structure, and was a garden in name only. Located on Madison Square just north of 26th Street in Manhattan and created by the famous showman P. T. Barnum, it was an arena, a cavernous building that had once housed the New York terminus of the Grand Central Railroad before that terminus was moved to East 42nd Street. In 1890, Stanford White, the most celebrated architect of his time, designed a newer Garden on the site to take the place of the old structure. This Madison Square Garden enclosed the largest arena in the world, and it remained on the site until 1924. After hosting that year's Democratic National Convention, it was torn down and a new Madison Square Garden was erected by a boxing promoter in another location in Manhattan, at the western edge of the Broadway theater district, taking up the entire city block bounded by 49th and 50th Streets and Eighth and Ninth Avenues. That midtown Garden became the locale for many sporting events, rodeos, and circuses, and in the early 1960s was even the setting for a gala honoring President John F. Kennedy at which

*Our construction division's first project for an outside firm,*
*Madison Square Garden.*

Marilyn Monroe had famously sung "Happy Birthday." But by then
that structure had become antiquated, and Irving and Jack Felt, enter-
prising real estate brothers, made a deal to erect a new Madison Square
Garden above Pennsylvania Station at 33rd Street between Seventh
and Eighth Avenues.

A study showed that 90 percent of people who came to the Eighth
Avenue Garden did so by public transportation, and the Felts reasoned
that since two subway lines and the Long Island Railroad commuter
lines went through Penn Station, siting the new Garden at Penn Station
would mean even more business for the new facility.

In addition to the Garden, the complex was to include a linked
office tower known as Two Penn Plaza—linked, in that the basic equipment for the both buildings' heating and air-conditioning systems were
to be in the office building.

The Felts, real estate owner/brokers of long standing in the city,
had good connections to City Hall, and the combination of their deep

knowledge of the real estate market and their political savvy had produced the opportunity to create the new Madison Square Garden. As their architect for the Garden, they engaged Charles Luckman. Earlier, as the president of Lever Brothers, Luckman had had much to do in the designing of Lever House, the Lever Brothers' modern glass skyscraper headquarters on Park Avenue in New York; after that feat, Luckman had retired as a corporate executive and had once more taken up his first love, architecture.

As joint venture partners in the construction of the new Madison Square Garden, two other big players were involved: Turner Construction, a New York-based general contractor, and the Del Webb construction firm. Webb's firm was not only a well known general contracting firm in the West, but Webb himself was a recognized figure in the sports field, and was at that time a part owner of the New York Yankees.

The Tishman and Felt families knew one another well, both socially and through business, and that was how the Tishman Company came into the mix on the site, as a 25 percent owner of the Two Penn Plaza building, and as the Construction Manager for both buildings.

This was a marvelous opportunity for Tishman Realty, and for our construction division. For years, I had been agitating to my uncles and cousins to permit our division to construct projects for outside owners, but they had always said no. I had continued to argue that the more work we might do for other owners, the better chance we would have of attracting highly qualified construction professionals for those times when Tishman Realty required construction services for its own new buildings. Their argument back to me was that if my division did work for outsiders, it would end up paying less attention when working for Tishman Realty's interests. The argument did not resolve until the opportunity arose to work on Madison Square Garden.

If I had to pick a particular moment when Construction Management began, it would be this one. The Madison Square Garden and Two Penn Plaza project occasioned it. For my construction division, here was the chance to do both things at once, to work for Tishman

Realty and at the same time to work for other owners. Through discussions with the Felts we came to a structure for the construction division's participation that was basically a rental arrangement. In practice, this meant that during the Garden's design and construction, my colleagues and I as construction professionals were absorbed into the joint venture formed to build and manage the property, serving as that joint venture's construction advisor, advocate, and coordinator in working with the architect and contractors, on behalf of the owners.

That was the essence of Construction Management. I thought it was logical, and appropriate to the task at hand—Madison Square Garden and Two Penn Plaza. I was not aware of any other companies then working in a similar manner to supervise construction. The construction company Morse/Diesel had worked so closely with developer Erwin Wolfson that they had an effective partnership, but in our arrangement for MSG, my construction division would supervise the individual trade contractors and subcontractors for the developer as its agent, not be the contractor.

What the Construction Management arrangement meant for me was that I became involved every step of the way, starting with the basic decision of where to situate the Garden on the site; prior to our getting involved, the shell of the old Pennsylvania Station had been demolished, and the station's functions had been moved underground, to a level at which the railroad's terminus connected directly with New York's Seventh and Eighth Avenue subway lines. I was just as happy not to have been involved in the destruction of the old terminal, which had provoked a huge outcry from preservationists. Shortly, they would spur the creation of the New York City Landmarks Commission, chartered to prevent the tearing down of other architecturally and culturally significant buildings before their history and intrinsic importance had been assessed. Once the commission had been established, owners and developers had to obtain its permission before the removal or renovation of such historically important buildings.

Irving Felt was an entrepreneur in many fields. A whiz kid, after graduating the Wharton School of Finance at 19, in 1929, he went to work on Wall Street just months before the 1929 Crash. By the late 1930s, he was heading an investment firm, and in 1959, when he bought the rights to Madison Square Garden, he was the head of several corporations, including those that owned hotels and sporting venues. An opera-lover and philanthropist, he was very active in all sorts of fields. He imagined the new Madison Square Garden as his crowning project. He was proud that in an age when big sporting arenas were using funds from municipal and state governments to build their arenas, he was able to put together a major sports arena in Manhattan that was entirely financed by private investors, thus not creating any extra burden on taxpayers.

Attending meetings with Felt, Luckman, and the other principals I felt like somewhat of a pipsqueak, although I was certainly a seasoned construction professional with more than fifteen years in the business. Luckman threw around the term "vomitorium," as though we were all supposed to know what it meant. I didn't, but I kept my mouth shut. Eventually I found out by listening that the vomitorium was an old Roman term referring to the passages at the various seating levels of a coliseum, through which the spectators would pour into and out of their seats. The talk of the vomitorium had to do with a design challenge for the architect: how to move around large numbers of people quickly and safely. For instance, there were to be seven entrances to the Garden, and forty-four high-speed electric stairways capable of transporting 70,000 people in an hour. The Garden would hold 20,000 people at a time, and would do so in varying configurations. The arena would be changed according to the needs of the event; the configuration required for a rodeo or a circus would not be the same as it would for a hockey game or a boxing match.

Since the mechanicals for both the Garden and Two Penn Plaza, the large connected office building, were to be installed in the office tower, it had to be completed first. But since the buildings were to be linked mechanically, all the technical problems of the Garden also had to be considered and solved before its construction began. For instance, while the boilers and chillers for the heating and cooling were to be located in Two Penn Plaza, the fans that would distribute the heated or cooled air were to be up inside the innovative cable structure that supported the immense, circular roof of the Garden. Among the mechanicals was a new air-purifying system; its goal was to somewhat eliminate the tobacco haze (from puffing patrons) that had afflicted earlier Gardens. Cigar smoke and haze had gotten so thick, particularly at prize fights, that some patrons complained that they couldn't see the action through it. This same recycling machinery would also de-ionize the air so that dust and smoke particles wouldn't stick to patrons' clothing.

In constructing this large edifice over the railroads and subways, some 300 columns had to be threaded through the various occupied levels, down to the base of the tracks, sixty feet below ground level. The placement had to be done quite precisely and coordinated with the very busy train schedules, so as not to unduly delay or detour the 650 trains coming into and out of the station each day, or their tens of thousands of passengers. Was this difficult? Yes, but it was also routine, a given that we had to work around the regular schedules of the train station, as well as the throngs of commuters and the phalanxes of attendants working in the Garden and pedestrians on adjacent streets. So we factored in the crowds and their needs in considering and coordinating the basic design of the project as well as in the construction procedures and deliveries of materials.

The most unusual feature of the Garden, from a design and construction point of view, was a cabled roof that would be column-free and this permit unobstructed views at all seating levels of the arena. Most arenas had truss-supported roofs, with exposed columns supporting the trusses. Such columns, of course, invariably cut off sight lines—that, too, had been a big problem in the 50th Street Madison Square Garden.

So the cabled roof was necessary in the new Garden; and above the cables and below the massive circular roof was the area that would house the exhaust fans and related equipment for the ventilation and air-conditioning systems.

Another interesting design feature—though not a particular challenge in construction—was a change in the location of the balconies.

The architects wanted the balconies recessed, not out over the arena as they had been in the previous Garden. Whereas the forward balconies at the midtown Madison Square Garden had permitted and sort of encouraged spectators to throw objects at players and performers they disliked, Felt wanted to prevent that from happening in the new Garden by setting the balconies back farther from the floor of the arena.

Though our construction division had never before been involved in the creation of an arena, it did not present technical problems beyond our experience or competence, and it was completed to everyone's satisfaction.

Our successful work with Madison Square Garden enabled me to better advocate to my family that our construction division should actively seek work as Construction Managers with outside clients to augment the work that we regularly did for Tishman Realty projects. Now, they agreed.

It was this understanding, and our track record in managing construction, that within a few years would lead our department to supervise $1 billion in construction projects annually, and to manage the building of the first three 100-story towers ever erected, which were at that time the tallest buildings in the world. In all these projects, we continued the model of the business arrangement created for the MSG complex: our construction department effectively became an agent of the owner. In that role, the project designers and trades accepted us as though we were the owner's in-house construction department, and we supervised every aspect of the project, from design through to completion.

## Gateway Center, Chicago

By the 1960s, partly because development opportunities in New York City were increasingly limited and because the suburbs were not attractive to us as sites for buildings, the Tishman Realty activities expanded by developing in other big cities such as Chicago and Los Angeles, and we were becoming known in those cities.

A new Chicago development opportunity for us at Tishman Realty arose, in a roundabout way, from Erwin Wolfson, one of the country's most interesting developers. In the 1920s, after taking a college degree in philosophy, Wolfson had invested in Florida real estate, making a lot of money in Florida before losing it all in the 1929 Crash; he then returned to New York and began again as an assistant timekeeper on a construction site. By 1936, he and a partner formed the Diesel construction firm, later Morse/Diesel. With Morse/Diesel as his construction arm, Wolfson had returned to development and over the next quarter-century erected more buildings in New York City than any other firm. The crowning one was the Pan Am Building, atop Grand Central Station in New York City, completed in 1960. Pursuing similar properties in other major cities, Wolfson had acquired the air rights to construct another over-the-rails complex in Chicago. After obtaining those rights, however, Wolfson was diagnosed with cancer and the prognosis was very bad. To maximize his estate for his heirs, he sold his development air rights in that Chicago parcel to Tishman Realty.

We planned to ultimately erect four buildings within those air rights, two of them immediately, and two more to follow if the location proved desirable to tenants. The construction would have to be carried out while 100,000 commuters daily would make their way into and out of the city via the Illinois Central rail lines directly beneath our work, but by then we knew how to do such things, since we had had to construct the new Madison Square Garden over the Pennsylvania Railroad and Long Island Rail Road tracks while dealing with tens of thousands of daily commuters and "sidewalk superintendents."

Because of the project's complexity, I decided that we ought to hire Chicago-based architects for the job, and called in the famed architectural firm, Skidmore Owings and Merrill. It had become a national firm with offices in many cities including New York, but still had its largest office in Chicago.

SOM was known as a "signature building" firm—one used by universities, institutions, and corporations to design structures that were visually striking and that looked good on the cover of a brochure but that did not necessarily have to be commercially viable. SOM was more design-oriented than commercially practical. I met with Bill Hartman, the head of the firm, and with Bruce Graham, the senior design partner at the Chicago office.

Bruce, who would later become known as Chicago's premier architect, had already completed three notable buildings in the city: the Inland Steel Building, which had exterior steel columns, the Equitable Building, and the Chicago Civic Center. I wanted to have him and SOM as our architects for what would be known as Gateway Center. However, I must have sounded so tough-minded about costs that Bruce and Bill were reluctant to commit the SOM firm to our project, arguing to me, "If you hire us, it'll probably be for only this one project and you'll never use us again."

They knew that their reputation was for being mostly interested in design and not in the practical aspects and costs of a "commercial" project. After all, they had been the architects for many innovative corporate headquarter buildings notable for striking imagery—and high cost.

"Yes, we'll hire you again," I said, "if you'll work with us to achieve a practical office building that will attract tenants." I explained that our buildings would have to have a variety of floor layouts, for instance, some for tenants who wanted negotiated rates, which really meant the lowest rates possible.

I emphasized that our funding for the project would have to be put into the practicality of the spaces rather than into the façades that might look good on the cover of their SOM brochure. Of course we also needed a design that would be attractive, but the greater need was for a design that would also allow us to rent the building profitably in a highly competitive market. We had to compete with other office buildings in Chicago's Loop area for commercial tenants, and couldn't price ourselves out of the competition by running up overly high construction costs. Would they be able to meet our requirements?

Graham pledged that they would, and I hired them on the spot.

SOM took to the challenge well, and we worked together to make a design that was both practical and good-looking. To begin with, there would be two twenty-one-story twin office buildings, and plans would be sketched for a third, to be finished a few years later. Today, Gateway Center has five buildings, extending for four blocks and adjacent to the river.

Construction had begun on the first two Gateway Center buildings when something interesting happened.

Our track record always helped us obtain new projects. But I must add that in my life, opportunities seem to have cropped up as much by chance as by design, and to take me and our firm in new directions that led to still further opportunities and interesting projects. That is precisely what occurred when, during construction of Gateway Center, I received an unexpected call from Bruce Graham. He informed me that SOM was interested in bringing us into an exciting project that his office was designing for another client.

## *Wolman and Hancock*

The SOM client was Jerry Wolman, and, as Jerry would be the first to admit, he was a neophyte in the construction of high-rise projects. He was a hearty laugher and liked joking around. He and his family had made money in a hardware store and taxicabs in Baltimore and Philadelphia, and in 1963 he had become the owner of the Philadelphia Eagles football team. Later on, he would be a founding owner of the Philadelphia Flyers of the National Hockey League.

According to Bruce Graham, Jerry Wolman had a handshake deal with the John Hancock Mutual Life Insurance Company to construct an "icon" building in their name on a very large site on Michigan Avenue in Chicago. Originally the building was to be eighty stories tall, but Bruce Graham had talked Jerry into building it taller—into making it 100 stories, which would then be the world's tallest. This was going to be a multiple-use building, commercial shopping and offices in the lower half, apartments in the top half, and perhaps it was the compel-

*Chicago's Hancock Tower—the world's first hundred-story building.*
*We served as its Construction Managers.*

ling need to make the whole project commercially viable that spurred Graham to recommend us to build it.

Beyond the two key facts—the 100 stories and the mixed use—the building had yet to be designed. That unfinished status was more than fine with me; we preferred being in on the design phase of all projects that we were to construct. The design phase is the period during which a project's design and practicality can be most affected positively or ruined. At Bruce's invitation, I went to a meeting in his office within SOM's New York headquarters. Bruce Graham, Jerry Wolman and I, just the three of us, met for about a half hour and before I left I had a handshake agreement to build the project.

The first and only 100-story building in the world! This was a wonderful assignment, and I looked forward to it, though not without some misgivings. Having listened to Jerry Wolman's admissions of not knowing much about real estate development, financing, or construction, I wondered whether the project would ever get off the ground. But a key fact emerged from our discussion: he had secured financing for the construction from the John Hancock Mutual Life Insurance Company. This had been done with a somewhat complicated arrangement wherein Hancock put up $6 million to buy the site, then leased it back to Wolman. A shrewd and sophisticated transaction, it gave me some assurance that the costs of construction would be met.

But I still had some doubts about the seriousness of this Wolman project, which were heightened by the results of a meeting that Jerry had asked me to set up in my office to go over the details of our relationship and his firm's relationship with Hancock. He, his lawyer, and another colleague, Jerry informed me, would be coming to New York from Philadelphia, and he stressed that we needed to be prompt, as they had other meetings scheduled for later in the day. I was there at ten, and so were his lawyer and his colleague, having taken a train from Philadelphia. But Jerry was nowhere to be found—these were the days before mobile phones. Jerry arrived after eleven. He had actually come to New York the night before, and on his way to my office from the Plaza Hotel—six blocks up Fifth Avenue, at the edge of Central Park— he had seen a lineup of horses and carriages and had decided he would take a short carriage ride. The driver, thinking he wanted the standard sightseeing trip, took him for a several-mile circuit around the Park before delivering him to 666 Fifth Avenue.

I became even more nervous when I learned, through the rumor mill, that despite our handshake deal, Jerry was now talking to our competitor, Turner Construction, about the Hancock tower. Bruce Graham was trying to head that off, and had convinced Jerry to at least speak with me again in person before reneging on our deal.

Around that time, I was the chairman of a charity fund-raising dinner—my title was more an honorific than an actual executive one—and we had a fund-raiser at which the entertainment was provided by a double-talker, the famous Professor Irwin Corey. He spoke so rapidly, and with such conviction, that he could easily convince you he knew what he was talking about, yet what he was actually saying was gibberish. Corey was fantastic. I laughed my head off. A few days later, when I learned that Jerry Wolman was thinking about reneging, I decided to set up a verbal sting operation. I asked Wolman if he would drop by my office when he was next in New York, and when the date was set I hired Professor Corey.

As Jerry sat down in my office, I told him that I'd heard the rumor that he was talking to another firm, and asked him what we could do to convince him again that we would be the best firm for his project. Then my phone rang and I picked it up; after a few seconds, I told Jerry that the call was for him, from the Turner Company.

Wolman got on the line and Irwin Corey began to give him a double-talk spiel about how the Turner Company was a better choice to build his Chicago project. Wolman fell for it, hook, line, and sinker—at first. Then, after a lengthy diatribe about Turner's superior services in Chicago, it finally dawned on Wolman that this was a practical joke. A good laugher, he seemed quite amused. I then had the "Professor" come in—he had been hidden away, a few offices down the hall—and we all had a good chuckle over it. I underlined for Jerry my more serious point: that we worked from an owner's *and* from a builder's perspective, and therefore could serve Jerry better than could a pure general contractor with little ownership experience.

That meeting sealed our deal.

# The Problem Caisson

Wolman's 100-story skyscraper was then going to be the tallest building in the world, and because the tower would be so high, a series of ten-to-twelve-foot-diameter caissons, the supports for the structure, had to be drilled into the ground to a depth of about 100 feet. The caissons were to be dug and filled with concrete even before the entire design for the building was complete, because no matter how the designs for the upper structure progressed, the caissons would have to be emplaced in expectation of the sizable loads that would need to be supported. Our experience enabled us to push the process along on a "fast track" schedule. SOM had insisted on the right to inspect and oversee all the work, including the caisson work. Usually we would do that by employing an independent consultant, but SOM had emphasized to Wolman that inspection was their province, a service that larger architectural firms provided to clients, for which they charged a site inspection fee.

As the caissons were being poured, SOM reported no problems with them, but one of our men on a routine trip around the site discovered that one caisson had sunk about a foot below the height it had been the night before. This was bad news—big, bad news. All work on the site had to be stopped. Some of the superstructure steel had already been erected, but further steel deliveries had to be held back while all the caissons across the entire site were inspected. The testing process took several weeks, since the only way to check whether any other caissons might have similar problems was to core-drill through *each one's* already hardened concrete to the bottom. The process was expensive, time-consuming, and frustrating.

A void in the problem caisson had opened in the concrete, and had caused the concrete above the void to sink of its own weight. But no one could come up with a definitive explanation for how a "slug" of concrete, ten feet in diameter and one foot thick inside the caisson, could have slipped sideways and disappeared. The reason could have been the building's location, close to the edge of Lake Michigan. It could also have been the quality of the concrete, or the way in which the concrete had been poured, or it could have been attributed to a couple of other causes. All of us were unable to figure it out, and while we tried to do so and tested every single other caisson, the cost of not continuing to build was mounting. All tests done on the caissons across the site came up negative—there was nothing wrong with the other caissons. Eventually, the void in the first one was filled with new concrete, and we were able to go ahead with the construction.

The various parties sued over their losses incurred due to the faulty caisson, but they couldn't sue us because we had not taken on the obligation to inspect the work on the site. That had been by contract SOM's bailiwick, and so they had to defend themselves legally against the claim that proper inspection would have caught the problem while the concrete was being installed, and prevented the losses due to having to remedy the caisson problem.

Thereafter, on other jobs, I would readily accept that the architect or an independent engineering firm would do all on-site inspections on jobs we were building, since the fees that we would have been paid for this inspection service were not worth the risk of litigation that might ensue if a similar problem developed and was not caught by job the site inspectors. Even so, since the problem caisson in Chicago had been on "our" site, some of the blame for it became affixed to us. For years afterward, I would be asked questions from inside the industry and from the media as to whether we had been at fault in this caisson business. We weren't, but it remained a difficult implied allegation to shake.

## The Sky Lobby and the X's

One of the innovative design features of this first 100-story building was dubbed the sky lobby. In tall buildings, elevator shafts can fill extraordinary amounts of space—so much space that they severely limit the available rental or salable floor space. SOM addressed this problem with the then-unusual idea of a sky lobby, coupled with two series of elevators rather than one. Rather than have a giant complex of elevators taking up floor space at every level, the amount of space devoted to a total of 47 elevators was cut down considerably. One set of elevators, the "express" elevators, would take large groups of people from the entrance lobby to the forty-fourth floor. Then two other sets of "local" elevators would take them farther. One of these sets went from forty-five to sixty-five, and another skipped those floors and served the floors above sixty-five. (Only a few elevator shafts went directly from the main lobby floor to the building's top-floor restaurant.) The express elevators were giants, capable of holding 10,000 pounds, and of traveling at speeds up to 1,600 feet a minute—almost a third of a mile in a minute.

The sky lobby floor, the forty-fourth, was also the dividing line between the commercial spaces below and the residential apartments above. So on that floor there was a pool, a gym, a dry cleaner, a convenience store, mailboxes, a library, a barbershop, a drugstore, and other amenities of a small city's Main Street. On election days, residents could even vote there.

The building tapered as it went upward, a very dramatic and interesting shape. Its final height was just a few feet shorter than the Empire State Building—because local zoning regulations and federal aviation restrictions would not permit it to be any taller. Still, it was the world's first 100-story building.

Another very intriguing design element was visible from inside and out, the huge X-shaped cross-bracing on the building's exterior, over the bronze-tinted glass windows. Some residences and office spaces had their windows partially blocked by the steel members that crisscrossed outside the glass, but that was only in some of the windows. The "X-bracing," as it was known, allowed more structural strength and flexibility. It both shored up the exterior and freed space in the interiors. The idea of exhibiting rather than hiding the structural elements was a long-time Chicago architectural tradition, part of the Mies van der Rohe "structural expressionist" style that was translated into the building's design by SOM structural engineer Fazlur Khan, one of my most admired and favorite professionals. Years later, the 100-story tower would be affirmed by architecture enthusiasts as being among the most distinctive buildings in the world. Architectural historian Paul Goldberger, in *The Skyscraper*, described the building as "a tall shaft that narrowed on all four sides as it moved toward the top. It proudly, almost arrogantly, displayed its structural reinforcements— huge X-braces cutting across the façade. It was a building of swagger, of enormous strength."

Because of the delay with the caissons, and other unrelated real estate matters that had nothing to do with the pace of construction, Wolman got into financial trouble quite early in the construction phase. He was involved in so many other interests—mainly his sports teams—that he was finally forced to let the Chicago tower go, at a loss that the media estimated at $5 million. The Hancock Company, the lender on the project, took over the unfinished building and decided that the company's image would be helped by having its name on the building, and so the 100-story tower became the John Hancock Center. Indeed, within a few years, Hancock was able to document that the association of the company with the tower that dominated the Chicago skyline did sell significantly more insurance policies in the geographic area. It was also a good real estate investment whose apartments rented well because they had spectacular views. I always liked the advertisement for the building that said, "Live uptown … work downtown. You can commute by elevator in seconds."

After Jerry Wolman's money problems, he also came out of the project okay. Paying most of his attention to the Philadelphia Eagles, he was eventually able to sell his interest in the team for three times what he paid for it. Since then, he has successfully developed many real estate properties around the country.

## Three that We Didn't Do

Irving Felt had landed a big opportunity: he had convinced Baron Rothschild that in order to maximize the worth of his family's property in Paris, he should build a Madison Square Garden arena on its front lawn, where it would become the headquarters of television production for France and possibly for all of Europe. Charles Luckman was also involved. Before any planning could be started, we sent our project managers to the site to scout out whether the parcel of land was of adequate size for such a large-scale building. Then I was invited to come to Paris for a weekend, with my wife, along with Felt and Luckman and their wives, to attend a meeting with Baron Rothschild in his chateau. Susan and I went, and we had a glorious dinner and luxuriated in a grand hotel. Then Luckman arrived, looking green from food poisoning. Felt was the last to arrive, looking exhausted from a night out with a "lady friend." Next morning when the meeting took place, in an impressive living room of the mansion, where we were served coffee around an equally impressive table, Felt and Luckman were out of it. That left me, the youngest man in the room, to face Baron Rothschild. I made a game presentation, but determined right away that the baron's enthusiasm for the project had been sapped by the unavailability of the senior men and also because he was not keen on having a facility for the masses in his front yard. Additionally, our scouts had determined that the site was too small for the intended size of the Madison Square Garden de Paris. Needless to say, this project never got off the ground.

During our time in Chicago, Sears Roebuck, then a giant retailer, wanted to erect a building in downtown Chicago so that they could move in town from their current headquarters, which was then way out in a suburb. Seeking something architecturally significant, they sought to engage SOM as their architect. But we had an agreement with SOM that prohibited the firm from accepting a project in competition with our Gateway Center project until we completed all of our Gateway development. Bruce Graham came to see me to ask whether SOM could get a release from our agreement. By this time we were friends, and I was inclined to grant this favor. But when he came to ask it, he did not know that we were simultaneously talking to Sears to persuade them to build their new headquarters on our Gateway Center site, which was directly across the Chicago River and only about a block from the site that SOM's client was offering to Sears. The fact that we were talking directly to Sears would clearly have precluded SOM from being able to accept the Sears commission.

However, we allowed him to make a proposal for the developer, who ultimately won the right to put the Sears Tower on his site. There was an additional conflict, however, which we did not discover until later, and might have changed our mind, had we known about it at the time of the waiver: the broker on whom we were relying to sell our site to Sears was also pushing the competing site.

So the Sears Tower went ahead without us, and is considered one of Bruce's most significant architectural designs. It might have competed somewhat with Gateway Center, but our property was finished ahead of the Sears Tower and we were well-rented and commercially viable by the time that Tower was ready.

Although the Hancock Center was in Chicago, the Hancock Company's corporate headquarters was in Boston, and they soon decided to build a Hancock Tower in Boston—and to choose another construction company rather than ours to handle the job.

I can't exactly say that made me unhappy, because we always wanted to be in on large projects, but Hancock's Boston site proved to be even more difficult than the Chicago one, and there were many costly delays and problems in its construction. We might have been able to foresee and avoid those problems, which were largely attributable to the site's underground conditions, but then again, we might not have. I never regretted not being involved in that project

## Fear of Heights, but Not While Flying

Having acrophobia, a fear of heights, I never liked to get too close to the edge of high buildings or even to go out on a floor during construction when the outside wall had not been installed. By the time we worked on the Hancock Center, I had become a pilot and regularly flew small planes; I had no fear of being in the air if I was at the controls of the plane. As a student pilot, I even had to do spins and other near-acrobatic maneuvers, which never bothered me as much as going near the edge of a high-rise floor under construction. Learning to fly in the late 1940s, I was taught in a canvas-covered, single engine, very low-powered Piper Cub based in the Hudson River. The plane could not climb well immediately after takeoff, and I would often have to fly *under* the George Washington Bridge until I could gather enough speed to take the plane up to a cruising height. In those days, to obtain a license you were required to be able to put your plane into a spin and, of course, to come out of it—a maneuver that could easily have induced my acrophobia to take over, but didn't. Today, planes are manufactured so that they resist going into a spin, and pilots no longer have to demonstrate their competence in that aspect of flying.

When I traveled upward in construction hoists on our building sites, especially in the higher structures, I had to conquer my acrophobia, or at least push it out of my mind and appear brave. I did. Sometimes I would take a few visitors up by the hoists, and when on top they would cling to the core of the building or to the penthouse, if it had been constructed, not wanting to let go for fear they would be swept over the side and fall to their deaths. I, too, had that fear, but worked assiduously at pretending that there was nothing to be afraid of. I never fell, and neither did my visitors.

Flying on the weekends was my relaxation. I loved it, and for fifty years flew my own plane, steadily getting myself licensed on larger and more complicated aircraft. Occasionally I would take my plane to visit construction sites. One of my favorite weekend destinations was Atlantic City, where over time we had several job sites. I even flew there long after our projects had been completed, to enjoy a weekend of food and entertainment at one of the casinos we had built.

*Flying my own plane was my avocation and my joy.*

## Conceiving a World Trade Center

The idea for a World Trade Center near the southern tip of Manhattan was born in the era after World War II, but really started moving in the middle 1950s, when the Port Authority of New York and New Jersey took charge of the notion. David Rockefeller, then president of the Chase bank, and his brother Nelson, governor of New York, championed the notion, but the man who really ran with it was Austin Tobin, who had been the executive director of the PA since 1942. The Rockefellers commissioned a study by SOM of lower Manhattan, and in 1960 SOM came up with a development that would be spread over thirteen acres near Wall Street and would encompass many buildings, some of them quite tall. This plan was somewhat patterned after that of the three other complexes that the Rockefellers had helped develop over the years, Rockefeller Center, the United Nations, and Lincoln Center. The PA took over this plan, got a few more architects involved, and in 1961 came up with a twin-towered centerpiece of the complex that would provide more than 10 million square feet of office and exhibition space. The hope was that this development would revitalize the downtown area.

The project entailed sealing off five streets and evicting hundreds of businesses. It was also controversial because the World Trade Center towers would compete for commercial tenants with buildings erected by private developers and because it was publicly funded, would be able to undercut the prices that private developers could offer to tenants. The PA had the right of eminent domain—to buy, condemn, and tear down buildings in the service of a public goal, and to do so despite the objections of the current property owners. The PA also had lots of money, and more pouring in every second, because it controlled most of the access routes into Manhattan—the bridges and tunnels, which were producing toll receipts in the tens of millions of dollars each month, as well as bus terminals at the Manhattan exit of the Lincoln Tunnel and the George Washington Bridge, the destinations of massive numbers of commuter buses each day. Governor Robert Meyner of New Jersey pushed Tobin to include in any lower Manhattan design a terminal for rail transport from New Jersey, the PATH—Port Authority Trans-Hudson line. The governor who succeeded Meyner, Richard Hughes, demanded that the PA do even more for New Jersey in the plan, and the PA then agreed to construct new PATH stations on the Jersey side of the Hudson.

By the end of 1961, the entire enterprise and use of the site had the approval of both governors, and of James Felt, then the New York City Planning Commission chief, and was ready to go.

After that, things became complicated, with staunch opposition from Mayor Robert F. Wagner of New York City, who was miffed because he had not been properly consulted, and from the occupants of the more than 150 buildings in the area, mostly small shops and businesses, buildings that were going to be razed so that the World Trade Center buildings could be erected on the site.

But the project went forward. Minoru Yamasaki was appointed as the architect, to be assisted by the Emery Roth & Sons architectural firm. The Yamasaki firm would design the exterior concepts and models, while the Roth firm—long a mainstay of commercial developers in the city—would

*Tishman Construction served as Manager for the Port Authority of New York and New Jersey for the original World Trade Center towers.*

do all the interior layouts, detailed drawings, and construction documents. Yamasaki was the hot architect of the moment, having recently shot to prominence with designs for a synagogue in suburban Chicago, the 1962 Seattle World's Fair, a building at Harvard, and a skyscraper in Detroit.

Before the architects and designers became involved, the site had to be readied, and the PA undertook to solve its inherent problems. The western part, nearest the Hudson River, was saturated with water beneath the surface, since much of it had been filled with various junk and excavated material that had been taken from all over Manhattan, through the centuries, as the island had become more and more developed. A "bathtub" needed to be created to keep out the groundwater and to provide a firm foundation. The tub walls were formed and poured in 152 sections covering about four square blocks, an enormous area. The material taken out to create "the tub," about a million cubic yards, was then used as fill to help create twenty-eight acres of land in the Hudson River, adjacent to the site, on which Battery Park City and the World Financial Center were later erected. After the proposed WTC site had thus been cleared of water, design and construction could begin—and that's when we got involved.

## Landing the Job

The PA decided to build the Towers and the surrounding buildings in phases, and to first award a contract only for the preconstruction phase of the towers. The designs and such were submitted for evaluation and critique to four firms, the Fuller and Turner construction firms, the Morse/Diesel firm, and us. Of these firms, Morse/Diesel was the most like us—a company that built for its own developing arm and also for other owners—while the Fuller and Turner firms were straight general contractors. As it happened, Fuller and Turner, the two largest GC firms in the country, had friends among the PA's commissioners, some of whom were heads of banks and corporations who had hired those firms in the past. The plans for the towers were still fairly preliminary, so we had an opportunity to critique the design assumptions of the planning, and did so from an owner's perspective. There were to be two square, 100-story buildings, each with floors about one acre in size—a structure quite different from the Hancock's tapered shape.

We made several key suggestions. The first and perhaps the most important was to recommend changing the location of the air-conditioning equipment and related mechanical systems. Yamasaki and

Roth had placed these at the top of each tower. From our perspective, derived not only from our experience with the Hancock Center but from the office buildings we had built and operated for ourselves, placing the equipment on top of the buildings would be economically disastrous, as it would require each tower to be "topped off" before the boilers and air conditioning equipment could even start to be installed. Doing the mechanicals in that sequence would delay tenant occupancies by as much as a year—a year during which the Port Authority would be denied rental income. However, by alternately placing the basic mechanical equipment, consisting of massive chillers and boilers, at the bottom of the towers, it would be possible to have those systems up and running long before we topped off the building, which would make occupancy of some lower office spaces possible even before completion of all the upper floors. This change would provide the PA with tens of millions of dollars in early rental income.

Our second-most important suggestion had to do with how and when construction materials were to be brought into the buildings. The width of the building's windows was to be unusually small, just eighteen inches wide; the reason for such a small width was to ensure that a person looking through a window from an upper floor would not feel that he or she was in danger of falling out. This design feature controlled the over-all structural pattern: a steel cage in which the open spaces would be the windows. What the architects had not figured into the design was that the small window size would prevent materials such as plasterboard and ductwork, being brought into the building by cranes. In other words, the design would seriously hamper construction. We suggested that a minor change could make construction easier: the corners of the towers could be "splayed," instead of at 90-degree angles, as the architect's plan called for. This splaying would open a wider area into which materials could be inserted.

Both of these changes were adopted.

Austin Tobin was known as an autocrat, polished and sophisticated but also very rough on his subordinates and on those wanting anything from the PA. However, with me he was always very considerate and respectful, and treated me very well, perhaps because he appreciated that we were trying our best to apply our owner/builder experience to his project and to help him save time and money. Our Construction Management approach constituted a new method for the PA, one contrary to Tobin's experience of hiring "lowest bidder" general contractors. With GC's, the Port Authority had always had to argue over claims for extras and for cost overruns caused by timing delays. Our CM approach would eliminate those headaches for him. He also sensed that I shared his excitement at being involved in his decade-long dream of erecting a World Trade Center. Tobin and the PA commissioners recognized the worth of the design changes that we proposed, and chose us to handle the pre-construction phase of the entire project. But there was a catch.

Because of all the pressure that Fuller and Turner were able to apply to the board of commissioners, the PA contract specifically stated that the firm selected for pre-construction must "terminate" its services after the pre-construction phase.

*To bring down the cost of the steel in the Towers, we divided up the work among eleven different firms.*

I was not willing to sign a contract with such a clause in it, but I wanted the job, so I sought some expert help in getting past this potential contract-killing clause.

Samuel I. Rosenman, a lawyer who had been a speechwriter for Presidents Roosevelt and Truman, was my neighbor and friend, and I asked him to assist me in having this contractual clause eliminated and a substitute written in that would allow us to be *considered* for the construction phase but that would meet the PA's requirements by not assuring us of being selected. The PA's original concept had been that at the end of the pre-construction phase, they would ask for bids on the second phase, the construction phase. To Tobin and the PA's chief of construction, Sam Rosenman and I argued that our taking the contract for the pre-construction advisory phase should not automatically preclude us from being considered to handle the construction phase and that our substitute clause would protect them and protect us. Eventually, they agreed.

I wasn't exactly pulling a fast one, but I knew, from two decades of construction, that the preproduction and production phases of construction would unavoidably overlap. Phase One would meld into Phase Two, and, I expected, the PA would simply see the benefit of keeping us on, as part of their team, through the construction phase.

## Nerves of Steel

Phase One would have to merge into Phase Two, I knew, in such matters as forward contracts for materials. The towers were going to be so large, and would use so much steel and other materials that these supplies would have to be contracted for and produced early on in order for them to be available in time for construction. The prime example was the contract for the structural steel. At the time, most tall buildings were built around steel superstructures, with vertical and horizontal steel beams and columns framing and supporting individual floors.

The columns were inside, so that the exterior did not have to hold up anything but the windowed "curtain" walls. For the World Trade Center towers, the approach was different: the support would be at the edges and at the center core. Horizontal trusses supported every floor, spanning from the outer columns to the core. The structure was a box within a box, the outer box or cage made up of fifty-nine steel columns spaced three feet apart, with windows in between; and the inner box, at the core, made of forty-seven columns housing the elevators, elevator lobbies, stairwells, and restrooms. This design gave the building great stability and horizontal resistance to wind as well as to the vertical force of gravity. The configuration also provided tenants with about three-quarters of an acre of column-free space per floor. The buildings were designed so that they could actually sway about three feet in the highest wind without cracking. To minimize the potential feeling of movement within the building, as well as the noise of slippage, some 10,000 visco-elastic dampers were installed between the floor structure and the outer walls.

So much steel had to be bought that it seemed there could be only two bidders, U.S. Steel and Bethlehem Steel, the country's largest steel suppliers and fabricators. In 1964, both companies had told the Port Authority that the cost would be around $82 million to supply and erect all the steel. But at the time of formal bidding, they submitted renewed estimates that were almost precisely the same, around $100 million, or $100 per ton.

As we approached a date of about a year prior to the expected need for the steel on site, we informed the PA that the award of structural steel contracts had to be made, as at least a year was needed for the bidding, for the fabrication, and for the transport and delivery of the fabricated steel. This, of course, was one of those construction-phase decisions that could not be put off until the awarding of a contract for general contractor. The PA recognized that truth and asked us to organize the bidding and negotiate the steel contract or contracts. We sent out requests for bids and the two giant companies came back with sealed bids that were almost exactly the same, $118.1 million for

Bethlehem, and $122.2 million for U.S. Steel, or more than $120 per ton, 20 percent more than their previous estimates.

Since the PA commissioners had already approved a budget of $100 million for steel, the steel giants' bids were unacceptable. What to do? The situation was exacerbated when critics of the proposed Trade Center towers learned of the bids and took out full-page newspaper advertisements saying, in effect, "The figures are shocking." And they were. It was obvious, to me and to many other people, that the two bidders had done some sharing of information, since these both came in at about 20 percent higher than their earlier bids although the work to be done hadn't changed.

Many components of the building were to be included in the steel contract: at least three types of steel, and two different processes—finishing and fabricating, and erecting. High-strength steel would be used at the base of the buildings, conventional-strength steel would go into the columns and beams, and trusses and other shaped panels would be made of other types of steel and by different fabrication methods. I knew that the big companies would have to subcontract out much of the work to smaller companies that specialized in these other types of steel or fabrications. So I suggested to Tobin that we go directly to such specialty suppliers and thereby eliminate the extra costs that U.S. Steel or Bethlehem were attempting to charge the PA for work they were not even going to perform in-house but would be paid, rather, for their "handling" the job.

My suggestion carried great weight with Tobin because he knew that Tishman Construction would not make any more or any less money, under our "fixed fee" arrangement, if the total cost of the steel were $20 million higher or $20 million lower. That underscored the purity of our argument, as well as our agreement with the Port Authority and our professional relationship with them.

Everyone expected great pushback from the commissioners to this idea of giving out the steel contract in pieces to smaller companies. One of the PA commissioners was a champion of Bethlehem Steel, and he was vehement that the contract should go to that company.

There was an additional potential problem that we understood only when our guys went around the country, soliciting bids from smaller steel fabricators, for instance, for the plates from a company that built ship hulls and Pullman cars on the West Coast, and for the high-strength harp-shaped façade steel from a company in Pittsburgh that specialized in it. Each potential bidder was wary because they did not want to bollix up their normal relationships with the big guys, who regularly gave them sizable orders. In order for these independent fabricators to accept the PA jobs, they needed some sort of protection from the giants, even though for many of these smaller companies the work for the Trade Center Towers would be the largest job they'd ever done. No fabricator wanted to be blackballed by Bethlehem or U.S. Steel. There was only one way to guarantee that they would not be blackballed: to deliberately exclude Bethlehem and U.S. Steel from further bids on the World Trade Center towers. And that is what the PA, with our assistance, did. This formulation was acceptable to Tobin because of the outlandishly high price of the giants' last bids, and because of the $40 million differential in the PA's favor between those bids and the ones we were able to tentatively solicit from the smaller companies. But it was only after we assured Tobin that the $40 million overage could be saved, and we had informed the smaller companies that Bethlehem and U.S. Steel would not be permitted to supply and erect the steel for the towers, that the independent specialty fabricators felt comfortable enough to bid. For the eleven elements of the job, the total aggregate of all these smaller company bids came to well under $100 million, precisely the amount that we had anticipated.

Tobin liked this arrangement, and so did John Skilling and Les Robertson, the structural engineers. Tobin now wanted me to present this steel purchase scenario to the Board of Governors.

It was a big day for me, the most significant presentation I'd ever made. I was still young, in my early forties. Most of the board agreed with my suggestion of bidding out the steel to the smaller fabricators. The Bethlehem-promoter did not. He asked, how can the PA trust

Tishman to deliver on budget? My answer should have been obvious to him, but I was glad to supply it: that we had no financial stake in the decision being made, and that we would not make one cent more or less, no matter what they chose to do, but going with the specialty contractors would save the project $40 million for the two towers. The PA board decided to do the bidding our way. Bethlehem Steel and U.S. Steel were shut out of the bidding, and eleven separate contracts were let for each unique structural portion of the steel required. The eventual cost of the fabricating *and erecting* the steel ended up at $96 million for each tower. Because there was so much steel to be used, and not enough room for it all on the site, the steel was shipped by rail to a point in New Jersey. There, each separate piece was tagged with a tracking number and only the correctly numbered pieces were delivered to the site by train or truck in a "just-in-time" delivery scheme.

There was never a second round of bidding for the handling of the construction phase of the WTC. Our pre-construction assignment just segued into the management of the overall construction, and we just kept on working, sending bills every month and getting them paid by the Port Authority. Tishman Construction was listed as "General Contractor" but we acted as Construction Managers and were paid a multiplier of the cost of all the supervisory personnel that we supplied to the project.

## The Elevators

Austin Tobin was a big-picture guy, not a hands-on manager. He preferred to have his subordinates do the detail work. For instance, a subordinate who was actually a PA commissioner himself was handling the bids for the elevators.

Yamasaki and Roth had adopted the sky lobby plan first used in the Hancock Center, although in the WTC Towers there was no natural division of lower and upper stories into commercial and residential as there had been in the Hancock. Large "shuttle" elevators would carry people to an intermediate floor, while one set of smaller elevators would service the floors above, and another would service those from the ground to that intermediate floor. The shuttles were to be the most capacious elevators ever used, able to accommodate fifty people (10,000 pounds). There was a limit to how fast such elevators could travel, because at an upward speed above 1,800 feet per minute your ears begin to pop and you feel g-forces in the way that astronauts do when they are rocketing toward outer space.

The designs called for "the largest vertical transportation system in history," as one report put it, including not only 200 elevators but an extended system of forty-nine escalators to take people between adjoining floors.

Otis and Westinghouse were the only possible bidders. I had done substantial projects with each of them. They had come in with bids that were, as with the steel companies, almost identical and higher than each had initially projected to the Port Authority months earlier. The PA was contemplating awarding the elevators in Building A to Otis and those in Building B to Westinghouse—but this made little sense to me. Elevators of the required size and speed had never previously been contemplated, and therefore, the engineering and other design features would have to be done from scratch by each of the two companies, which was perhaps why the estimated cost had gone up. Tobin asked me what the PA should do. I suggested that we select one or the other company, preferably the one with the most experience, and try to negotiate a favorable contract for the elevators for both towers. He informally asked me to see what I could do, and I told him that I would first try Otis. Tobin and I agreed on that, and also that no one in the Port Authority should know that I would be offering the work without going through the usual bidding process.

The next day I met, alone and on the sly, in a bar near my office, with Frank Wingate, a senior vice president and regional head of Otis, and offered him the contract for both towers at a price of less than 80 percent of the amount they and Westinghouse had "bid" a few days earlier. Otis soon agreed.

And so did Tobin.

This no-bid contract was a very unusual procedure for a public agency to indulge in and benefit from, but Austin Tobin was a strong leader, totally confident in his own decision-making. His willingness to go this unusual route gave me tremendous respect for him; moreover, his respect for me, which was inherent in his decision to let me negotiate and award this on my own, overwhelmed me with gratitude and pride.

## A Couple of Changes

Yamasaki had wanted for the façades of the twin towers, and of the other, smaller buildings surrounding the towers, to be made of stainless steel so that they would be shiny and reflective.

I thought this was unrealistic. We were able to show him and the PA that there were not enough stainless steel suppliers or specialized fabricators for this material anywhere on the globe, and that even if there were, the cost of using stainless steel would have been prohibitive. As an alternative, we suggested using aluminum. We then worked with Alcoa to make an anodized aluminum alloy that would provide the shiny and reflective qualities that the architect wanted, but would be lighter in weight than the steel and also more resistant to weather-produced deterioration. The chief worry, in that department, was of the corrosive qualities of salt coming from the nearby waters of the Atlantic Ocean—people don't realize the degree to which salt in the air can turn into acids that eat away at steel. The aluminum façade would be delivered in panels that were much lighter than steel panels, therefore easier to handle, and would be installed after the completion of each floor's interior construction.

New York City's building and fire codes were revised in 1968, and though these codes did not apply to the PA-owned buildings, the PA mandated that wherever possible these new codes had to be adhered to in constructing the Twin Towers. This meant, for example, that sprayed fire-resistant materials (SFRMs) were used throughout to protect the structural steel, beams and trusses. Gypsum fireproof wallboard in appropriate thicknesses was used in connection with SRFMs to protect the core columns.

Constructing the towers took several years, and was done in a remarkably even and problem-free manner, given the enormity of the project, the hundreds of subcontractors involved and intricacies of scheduling the storage and delivery of materials—and, of course, the need to work around the 100,000 people from New York, New Jersey and Connecticut who flowed into the area each morning and out of the area in late afternoon. Once again, we had to be expert and *very careful* in working around a major transportation hub and in preserving the safety of all the throngs of people above and around whom we were toiling. By now, after Madison Square Garden and the Gateway Center buildings in Chicago, no one in the construction field had more experience at working around throngs than we did.

As a big booster of prefabricated components, I negotiated their use for the World Trade Center towers with the various trade unions that had jurisdiction over such areas as electrical, plumbing, and phone-line installations. The fabricating of parts in a factory, rather than on site, allowed for greater quality control as well as for economies and greater speed. Prefabbed components could be stored off-site and delivered only when they were required and in a condition ready to be installed.

Because the mechanicals went in first, at the bottom of the buildings, the lower floors of the towers did become habitable well before completion of the far upper floors. The PA moved its offices into the North Tower in 1970, and for a while they were the only occupants of that building. The South Tower began to receive tenants in January of 1972.

## Ceremonies and Passings

The dedication ceremony for the World Trade Center towers was in April of 1973. For us, it had been five years of hard and sustained work, and I was happy to be there. But I was in shock because Austin Tobin had been forced out as director in 1972 after thirty years, and chose not to attend the ceremony. All of us who had dealt with him and had known intimately of his integrity and of his dedication to the creation of the World Trade Center were upset at the timing of this coup. I am certain that it contributed to his untimely death in 1978.

Early on, before we started the actual construction of the World Trade Center, a labor-union leader had shown up to picket outside our 666 Fifth Avenue headquarters. He and a group of construction workers stayed out there, day after day, handing out leaflets about the supposedly antilabor stances of our company. The allegations were not just against the company but against me personally, which angered and upset me because both I and the company took pride in being very pro-union, and in always using union labor on all of our construction works in New York and in all the other cities in which construction trade unions existed. From asking around, I learned that the target of this protesting was not really me or our firm, but rather was the World Trade Center project and especially the Port Authority, which had recently awarded some non-union contracts on parts of the work that they were doing themselves. The protester, and especially his picketing of our headquarters, drove Uncle Norman crazy.

Years later, I met the protester, and he told me that he had targeted our company, and particularly me, because he knew that I was pro-labor and that the protesting would get under my skin, and he had hoped that I might be able to persuade the Port Authority to award contracts on all of their projects solely to union contractors.

Some time after we had been awarded the World Trade Center project, Norman Tishman became very ill. He left the company entirely and was diagnosed with ALS, amyotrophic lateral sclerosis,

Lou Gehrig's disease, a fatal condition. He was bed-ridden in his apartment, and I went to see him there. He had never been noticeably enthusiastic or sympathetic toward the construction side of our company, had always been somewhat cool to me and oblivious of what I was doing. He was also a man who seldom gave out spontaneous compliments, especially in my direction. But during this deathbed session, he said he was very proud of me and of our construction division for landing the World Trade Center project. That meant a lot to me. Shortly after my visit, in 1967, Norman passed on, at age 65. His oldest surviving brother, David, thirteen years older, had retired and lived on. The leadership of Tishman Realty & Construction Company was now completely in the hands of the third generation, Bob, Alan, and myself.

*It was a great day when we completed the original Twin Towers, and they became a part of Manhattan's skyline.*

# FOUR

# Transitions

## The Family Breakfasts

During my early years with Tishman Realty, every weekday morning the Tishman clan would gather for breakfast before beginning work in the office. The locale of the breakfasts was the Lombardy Hotel, which was next to our then headquarters at 445 Park Avenue. I soon learned that the breakfasts were where the real issues of the company were supposed to be discussed. Because that was so, the attendees often included Uncle Alex and his two sons, who were not in the top echelon but wanted to feel as though they were or soon would be. I thought that was amusing, and was also a bit annoyed that these second-stringers would make it their business to be there, but I also recognized why they felt they needed to attend. I showed up at the daily family break-fasts because I didn't have a sponsoring father in the hierarchy, and if I had not been there, I certainly have been shut out learning important information about where the company was heading, and, more impor-tant, would not have been able to form an entirely separate operation under the banner of "The Tishman Construction Company."

When we moved into our 666 Fifth Avenue headquarters in 1957, the breakfasts were shifted to the Berkshire Hotel at 52nd and Madison.

Some time thereafter, I tired of the family breakfasts and stopped going to them, instead establishing another tradition of breakfasts with my senior construction colleagues at Stouffer's restaurant, on the first floor of the 666 building.

By the late 1960s, the family breakfasts were no longer being held, partially because all of my uncles were gone from the company, and the tradition went with them, but partly because my oldest cousin, Bob, was in charge, and he wasn't interested in the daily family confabs. Back then, we didn't call the top position in the company the CEO, but that's what Bob was. There were fewer Tishmans overall, since my cousins Bill and Peter had departed the company and my cousin Ed was solely devoted to property leasing and wasn't in the upper management.

Bob never questioned my judgment or my views, as my uncles had; he let me "do my thing," for instance, with the World Trade Center project. After all, Bob did not have sons who might compete with me, and he seemed to welcome my input in all aspects of the business, not just in those related to our construction activities. The corporation had evolved into three major divisions. Bob, assisted by his son-in-law Jerry Speyer, ran the real estate part of the enterprise, acquiring the land and making the financial deals connected with our portfolio of office buildings. Bob's brother Alan ran the management division, managing and leasing the office buildings that the family owned and operated. By this time, I was in sole charge of the construction division; we were then building for our own portfolio and, on a fee basis, for other developers and public entities, many of whose projects were substantial ones, such as the Hancock and World Trade Center towers.

The construction division was by far the largest part of the company in terms of number of employees and in taking up the largest amount of office space. It had a significant dollar income but most of that income flowed right back out again in salaries and overhead. The development sector was the smallest division in terms of number of employees, and although it was the division in which the big money could be made, it was also the source of our greatest exposure to risk. The management division had the second-largest contingent of employees, and a commensurate number of offices in our headquarter floors at the 666 Fifth Avenue building; it had more sources of income than our division but it made less money, but it did not have the upside potential that the development division and my construction division did.

However, we were all salaried employees of the public Tishman company, and that public structure began to be the subject of continual discussions among Bob, Alan, Jerry Speyer, and myself.

## The Public Company and Its Difficulties

In 1928, when my father had been alive and second in command to Uncle David, Tishman Realty & Construction had "gone public." As in the cliché, it seemed like a good idea at the time, a way to take advantage of the skyrocketing stock market and to properly assign a total value to the family's holdings. For a short while thereafter, everything sailed along just fine; the company owned a portfolio of luxury apartment buildings, mostly on upper Park Avenue, that produced a very good income stream from the rents. Other owner-builder families did not follow our example and go public; they remained as private, family-owned companies. Back then, being a public company seemed to be an advantage—your books were relatively open, which was attractive to underwriters, and the public reporting requirements permitted shareholders to see what you were doing and how. All this was fine when the economy was booming and the stock market was rising.

After the Crash of '29, being a public company in the real estate field was no longer such a good idea. Soon after the stock market collapsed, the once-wealthy tenants in the Park Avenue buildings had lost so much of their money that they became unable to pay their rent. During the 1930s, the stock market stayed down and it took the Tishman stock price down with it. However, to our set of shareholders the stock price of our company did not matter as much as did the stock price of, say, a manufacturing company mattered to its shareholders, since the major Tishman Company stockholders were our family members and their allies, who were neither buying nor selling shares.

After World War II, the equation changed once again. As pent-up demand for housing and offices led to a tremendous surge in erecting buildings, we made money, and the public-company structure was an appropriate configuration of ownership. But fifteen years after the end of World War II, when that postwar surge wound down, the public-company structure turned into an encumbrance.

What changed it from a plus to a minus were the advent of alterations in the tax code regarding how a building and its component parts could be depreciated and by whom. New laws permitted very rapid depreciation of a building and such parts of it as the elevators and other machinery, in ways that an *individual* could use to offset normal income and end up with huge savings because he or she would have to pay considerably less in personal income taxes. But only private developers and owners could reap the benefit of this rapid depreciation. Depreciation could still be applied for the benefit of a public company but not for its stockholders. The criterion for the depreciation schedule was the prospective life of the particular elements of a building; if the heating system had to be replaced every ten years, then it might be on a ten-year depreciation schedule, while the building itself had to be depreciated over many, many years. If you put in partitions for a tenant on a five-year lease, then you could depreciate those partitions over five years. The accelerated depreciation schedules were the parts of the tax code that provided the owners with the most important breaks.

The problem for the Tishman family was that the accelerated depreciation benefits for buildings could not be passed on to our stockholders, which negatively affected our major stockholders—including the family members who were running the company. When we looked at our investment in the public Tishman Realty company versus a similar potential investment with a privately owned developer, it became obvious we should go private. Until we did so, our public company would continue to be subject to a double whammy: not only could we not depreciate our buildings for our own and our stockholders' personal benefit, but our competitors as developers could, and the personal tax benefits made it possible for them to erect and rent their buildings at substantially lower prices per-square-foot than our company could afford to offer. This resulted in our being more than once faced with a situation in which we erected a building on a midtown corner only to have a competitor put up a similar building a block away, one that lured away our prospective tenants by offering them better deals. Over time, as the tax laws' accelerated depreciation benefits were phased in, our public corporate structure became more and more of a negative for us and for our major stockholders.

As the years rolled on into the early 1970s, the family tried to buy back all the extant shares owned by outsiders, but that did not work and so the public structure, and our family's percentage of outright owner-ship—about 35 percent—continued. We Tishmans may have held the largest block of stock, but Bob, Alan, Jerry and I were receiving only salaries, while our competitors, the chiefs of private companies, were putting up similar buildings to ours and becoming quite wealthy from their activities. In 1974, for example, the public company had to report a $38 million loss for the year, consisting mostly of depreciation; with such a loss, the company could not pay dividends to its stockholders. In 1975, we made a "bottom line" profit of just $1.8 million on gross revenues of $85 million. But our competitors, even in the downturn, were not faring as badly. Our bottom line was substantially worsened because of our white elephant, 1166 Avenue of the Americas, a build-ing that we had completed but that because of the downturn in real estate was not well-rented and was costing us millions of dollars each month in carrying costs. Eventually we had to allow the $100 million building to go into foreclosure; it was bought out of foreclosure by two pension funds and the New York Telephone Company, for $32 million— well below our cost, but at least we no longer had to bear the carrying charges.

Stocks in general were not hot, either. This was the era when the Dow Jones average hovered at around 1,000, and when many stocks were considered seriously undervalued. A 12.5-point one-day surge in the index was cause for a banner headline in *The New York Times*. In 1976, the building business in Manhattan was judged to have fallen to its lowest level since 1951.

Our internal discussions turned to the possibility of a sale of the company to some other concern, or of delisting, that is, of dissolving the public company. It turned out that the company was so large that it was unattractive to any corporate buyer, so we couldn't sell it. But we determined that our principal stockholders—the Crowns of Chicago, the Scheuers, ourselves, and other individuals—would fare better if we were to dissolve the public company, sell its assets, and re-form as a privately held company. This was a big step and not one to be taken lightly, so the decision was not reached overnight. Our major non-family stockholders, the Crowns and Scheuers, also vigorously expressed their desire to change the structure from a public company to a private one.

By the mid-1970s, Tishman Realty & Construction owned a portfolio of two dozen substantial office buildings. Over the years, some of our properties had been sold, for prime example, the 666 Fifth Avenue building that housed our headquarters. And now the project pipeline was growing thin—too thin to sustain the company. A major culprit responsible for that thinning pipeline, we knew, was the public structure of our company and the after-tax bottom line that translated into our having to offer rental properties at rates higher than those of our competitors.

The decision to delist hung fire for several years until a particularly favorable climate came about. A new regulation made it very attractive to sell all our properties very rapidly; if we could get rid of them all within one year, that would be considered a liquidation, a transaction on which there would be no capital gains tax imposed on the proceeds derived by the company. We agreed that we should liquidate, and began the process.

## Company For Sale

Evaluating the worth of the Tishman-owned buildings was relatively straightforward, since real estate values can be computed based on location, occupancy, current rent levels, and the like. Our portfolio was expected to sell for between $100 million and $150 million. Seventeen of the buildings would be bought as a package by the Equitable Life Insurance Company for $107 million. (Later, Lazard Realty would buy the rest for an additional $78 million.) Equitable also agreed to hire Alan's management division for the first five years to manage the buildings they purchased, so that division would live on as a unit of Equitable. But figuring out the value of the Tishman Construction Corp., the division that I had initiated and ran, was more complicated. The family decided to engage Morgan Stanley to provide an independent appraisal of the worth of the construction division.

The appraisal that Morgan Stanley rendered, of a bit more than $2 million, angered me, as I felt certain that this price seriously undervalued my division. I knew that a fee-for-service provider was more difficult to put a price on than were sunken assets like buildings, but this guess by Morgan Stanley was insultingly low. The figure offended me both as a Tishman stockholder and as the division's creator and chief. So I decided to take matters into my own hands. No one else in the family was particularly interested in what price my division would fetch, but they were most anxious to bundle the division with our real estate assets and sell it within the one-year window that would provide our stockholders with the greatest tax benefit. As an insider, I was prohibited by law from buying the division, and at that point in time I had neither the intention nor the wherewithal to buy it. But I had grown the division over the years, it was my baby, and I wanted to keep it intact.

So I walked across the street—literally—to Rockefeller Center, the headquarters of the Rockefeller empire, known as the Rockefeller Center Corporation. I had built for that division and knew its top people and they knew me and my team. The Rockefeller family empire was vast, with holdings in New York not only at Rockefeller Center but in other parts of the city, as well as in other areas of the world. I asked Alton G. Marshall, head of the Rockefeller Center Corporation, if that entity would be interested in buying our construction division, and what he thought the price ought to be. Al Marshall was a former chief of staff to Governor Nelson Rockefeller, a former chief of an important savings bank, and a man who knew his real estate. As the man in charge of running the whole Rockefeller Center complex, Marshall could value our service company in terms of its worth as a separate operating entity, and also in terms of its worth to Rockefeller to use for construction projects that Rockefeller already had in the pipeline.

Marshall immediately said that Rockefeller Center Corporation very well might be interested in buying our division. They had previously purchased the very large real estate brokerage firm Cushman & Wakefield, which had a division that advised clients on construction, and the Rockefeller pipeline contained many building projects for which a Rockefeller-owned construction division could be of great value. Once Marshall indicated Rockefeller Center Corporation's interest, I stopped looking for any other buyer. I wasn't interested in a competitive situation that would only slightly ramp up the price but that might bear with it some adverse consequences for me or my construction colleagues if someone other than Rockefeller bought us. I wanted a sale that would keep us intact and would allow us to continue doing what we had been successfully doing. By then, we had a reputation larger than we had once imagined possible, having recently built the three tallest buildings in the world, the 100-plus storied Hancock Center in Chicago and the two World Trade Center towers in New York.

I also wanted something else from the sale of the public company: I yearned to take the Tishman name, my division's distinctive logo, and the family legacy with me. To do so was a complicated task. The public Tishman company's residual obligations and liabilities had to be closed out, and there were other concerns. Rockefeller Center Group argued, and I concurred, that the name, logo, and corporate legacy were an integral part of their purchase price, a price to which I had agreed. This practice of including the logo and corporate history is generally called the "key," and ours featured the history of the Tishman family endeavors for the preceding seventy-five years.

The key was valuable because it bespoke continuity; and in construction, as in other professional services, your reputation and longevity in the business are very important; by bringing along the key I was stressing the qualities of continuity and integrity.

Without my insistence on retaining the key, and my understanding of its importance, the history and reputation of the Tishman name and brand might not have survived.

I also knew that as important as the key, to the future entity, was our group of highly talented and experienced colleagues, whom I considered to be the best in the business, the people who had had charge of erecting three of the world's tallest buildings.

We also had another asset, the long-term lease on two floors of 666 Fifth Avenue; the building was still known as the Tishman Building, although by that time it had been sold. We held a below-market-price lease that had another six or seven years to run, and was therefore very valuable in midtown Manhattan. Rockefeller was willing to project out, as Morgan Stanley seemed unwilling to do, how much income the construction division could bring in each year, a figure that had been on the rise for a while and that showed no signs of abating.

Claude Nash, the senior vice-president of the Rockefeller Group, Inc., who had been responsible for their acquisition of Cushman & Wakefield, did the numbers on acquiring our construction division and came up with a suggested purchase price of $7.5 million in cash, more than triple what Morgan Stanley had estimated. At the proposed purchase price of $7.5 million, I estimated, the construction division would pay for its own purchase within three years. Bob was away in Europe when this deal was struck, and when he found out about it, he said something to the effect that he couldn't understand how an engineer such as myself could triple what Morgan Stanley had set as a target price. He did not object to my selling the construction division, with its key, which included the name "Tishman Realty & Construction."

Because my division had by far the most employees, we needed the fully developed and furnished space in 666 Fifth Avenue and its below-market rent, and kept the lease as part of what was to be sold to the Rockefeller group. And so I was able to stay in the corner office that I had occupied since the building had been opened.

More than fifty years ago, my colleagues and I were the first people to move into 666 Fifth Avenue, and without question, we are the longest-in-residence inhabitants of the building. As I write this history, I am still sitting at the same desk, in that office. Now that's continuity!

In my discussions with the Rockefeller group at the time of the sale, we configured a relationship that would enable the construction division to operate mostly on its own, as we had been, and without managerial interference. Why tinker with a good thing? Sometimes the smartest action you can take is to leave well enough alone; as financier Bert Lance was then telling his friend, President Jimmy Carter, "If it ain't broke, don't fix it."

After I had presented Bob Tishman with the $7.5 million offer from the Rockefeller Center Corporation, the Tishman Corporation board members voted to accept it. (Of course I abstained from the vote.) Tishman Realty & Construction Co., Inc., became a subsidiary of the Rockefeller Center Corporation even before the Tishman corporation was delisted as a public company and dissolved. That happened after the majority of the corporation's assets—the seventeen office buildings—were sold to Equitable; thus the proceeds from that sale became part of the distribution to the stockholders.

The payout to Tishman shareholders from the proceeds of our various sales was far greater than they would have obtained by simply selling their shares of the public company on the stock market. However, due to the long-ago sale of half of my father's stock in the company, my immediate family received half the share of the proceeds from the dissolution of the old public company that was received by the children and grandchildren of my uncles. This smaller payout was an unpleasant reminder of times past, but I had no way of rectifying the situation and did not want to dwell on it, preferring to move forward.

The public Tishman Company ceased to exist, and its liabilities and obligations were completely gone—except for the name Tishman Realty & Construction, and its logos and its history, which were passed on to my group. Under our new arrangement, very little changed for the employees of the former Tishman-owned construction division. We continued to occupy the same offices, to have the original Tishman name on the door, and to continue to provide Construction Management services as we had done in the past. Only the ownership structure was new.

## The Three Tishman Entities

Three new entities had been set up. Alan Tishman's leasing and office management company had plenty to do from the get-go, continuing to administer the former Tishman properties now owned by Equitable. Robert Tishman and his son-in-law Jerry Speyer established Tishman Speyer Properties. For several years, they occupied offices alongside of my construction division in 666, paying us their pro rata share of the rent, until they constructed a building just down the block on 53rd (which we built for them) and moved to their own headquarters. Bob and Jerry continued the family associations with the Crowns and with the Equitable, who gave them a jump-start by investing heavily in the newly formed Tishman Speyer real estate company.

Our new entities and we three cousins got along reasonably well, but there were some sticking points between the construction entity that I headed and Tishman Speyer. Now a part of the Rockefeller Center Corporation, we were engaged by Tishman Speyer to erect their first two projects, and on site our construction people, as they had always done, wore Tishman Construction hard-hats, and our signs on the construction site fence and sidewalk bridges appeared to announce that this project was a Tishman Construction project. This signage made Bob, and particularly Jerry, quite uncomfortable, as they were at pains to establish the independent identity of their new firm.

An odd event occurred in this period just after the dissolution of the old public company. The public company had sold most of the extant properties as a portfolio, to Equitable, but a few parcels that were intended for development were disposed of separately. One was for a property in Newark, New Jersey, owned by the PSE&G utility. I heard through the grapevine that Tishman Speyer had made an offer seriously below market price for the development rights, and that the on-going public company board was about to accept the offer without competitive bidding. Since many Tishman family members, including me, and some non-family members were still substantial owners of the public company then being liquidated, I blew my top! What Tishman Speyer was offering was not, in my opinion, an appropriate price; if this deal went through as it was then configured, the public company's stockholders would receive a much lower distribution than they deserved. I quickly went to the Rockefeller interests, my division's new parent, and advised them to make a bid for the PSE&G property. They did, and the public company board had no choice but to accept it. Ultimately the price paid by Rockefeller was more than *ten times* what Tishman Speyer had offered, and the proceeds from the sale to Rockefeller made for an appropriate payout to the public Tishman company shareholders.

The shift on the sale of the PSE&G property was done very quietly, and without public attribution to me.

The Tishman Speyer attempt at obtaining the property by an inside deal was just a start-up mistake, and was never repeated. Soon Bob and Jerry's company was fully on the road to becoming what it is today, a colossus in the real estate development field with a terrific reputation for expertise and integrity.

## Under the Rockefeller Umbrella

We had several major projects awaiting as we began under the Rockefeller umbrella. For Rockefeller, we were constructing the Wells Fargo building in Los Angeles, and shortly, there was the PSE&G Newark property, which we fast-tracked. Our largest project though, was to be for The Disney Company, the EPCOT Center in Florida.

The full story of that remarkable construction task, and my long relationship with The Disney Company, is told in a following chapter. For the moment, let me quickly summarize it. We had been asked to be the Construction Managers for EPCOT, but construction had been delayed because of the oil shortage and then the zooming oil prices that were a result of the 1973 Middle East war, the Arab states' oil embargo, and price hikes by OPEC members. The Disney Company correctly assumed that in the face of high prices at the pump, Americans would cut down on their driving, and so they delayed construction of EPCOT. But they had wanted to have us continue to work within the Disney footprint in Florida, to hold the key people in place for the moment when EPCOT would begin, and so had asked us to take over construction of the second phase of the Polynesian Hotel in Disney World. That construction task occupied our employees and gave us plenty of experience in the Florida work environment, in which, in contrast to most other states, union and non-union workers would work together at a building site because Florida was a "right to work" state. What this meant in practice was that unionized workers entered through one gate of the work site, while the non-union ones went through another; once all of them had passed those gates, though, there was no further separation on the job-site, and were seldom any conflicts between the unionized and non-unionized workers. The Polynesian hotel construction was a good introduction for us to the ways of Disney, and of Disney to us.

Once EPCOT got going, I flew to California on a regular schedule to brief the Disney top executives on its progress. We had considerable latitude and responsibilities because many of the Disney construction chiefs were in Japan, supervising the construction of Tokyo Disney World. Disney did not have the depth of staff to supervise Tokyo and the project in Florida at the same time. (All of this was prior to the arrival at Disney of Michael Eisner and his partner, Frank Wells, which would complicate matters for me—but I'm getting ahead of my story.)

## When I Ran to Iran

During the period when the oil embargo was still affecting road travel, delaying the EPCOT construction, and the U.S. economy was in the doldrums, in order to keep our firm busy I looked for other construction assignments. It was obviously my task to find work for myself and my colleagues. That led, in a roundabout way, to a period during which, more than once—as I put it to friends—"I ran to Iran."

At about the same time, directly across the street from our head-quarters building, on the southwest corner of Fifth Avenue and 52nd Street, there was a site ripe for construction, and one day Congressman John Murphy, who happened to be a West Point graduate, accompanied by an Iranian gentleman, came to see me about it. The Pahlevi Foundation, an entity formed by the then-Shah of Iran, had decided to underwrite the construction of an office building on that site, and their American architect, John Carl Warnecke, thought it would be a good idea for them to ask us to provide an estimate of what the construction would cost.

For the Pahlevi Foundation, we examined and priced out the plans for the building across the street from our headquarters, and came up with an estimate on the construction of $23 million. I told this to the inquirers; they professed surprise, and asked me to travel to Iran and explain our budget estimate to the president of the Iranian senate, the second most powerful man in the country after the shah. I agreed to do so because we had recently opened an office in Tehran, as had many other construction companies in an attempt to find work during a slow period in the United States. I flew over on Pan Am, whose parent company also owned the Intercontinental Hotel. The airline had a regular round-the-world flight, their #1, that went from New York to Tehran and then across Asia and the Pacific before returning to New York.

As I had expected, I spent a lot of time in the lobby of the Intercontinental, awaiting calls to go see someone. In the lobbies of the Hilton and the Intercontinental were many other construction and development executives from other companies, several of whom I knew. Only later would we all learn that we were mostly chasing the same projects and had been promised the moon by the same architects and middlemen who, of course, claimed to have locks on their projects.

While in the lobby one day, I was paged. The pager was the representative of Jafar Sharif-Emani, then the prime minister of Iran, president of the Iranian senate and president of the Pahlavi Foundation. He wanted to see me right away, and had sent a limousine to take me to his office building. This was quite a prestigious thing to happen in Tehran, and in the lobby, heads turned. Reaching the office building, I was ushered into Sharif-Emani's massive and well-appointed room, in which he sat at a desk at the far end. As I approached the desk, I saw out of the corner of my eye a door opening a crack, and someone peering out from behind it.

I sat down in a chair in front of the desk, and was asked by Sharif-Emani for my estimate, which I provided. He expressed extreme surprise that it was so low. He told me that the architect and "others" had estimated the construction cost at $32 million. How could I be so certain that my $23 million estimate was correct? Because, I explained, we were New York-based, very experienced, and had regularly constructed office buildings on Fifth Avenue and therefore knew that our figures were current and accurate.

At this point the side door opened, and the Iranian intermediary whom I had met in New York appeared, and hurried in. He and the senate president had a conversation in Farsi, which I did not understand, and then I was hustled out of the office. After that, I never heard another word about the 52nd Street project, which was ultimately constructed by a New Jersey firm. I believe that the content of the conversation in Farsi was that the senator was informed that the extra $9 million, the difference between the $32 million and $23 million estimates, was destined for certain pockets, which I assume could well have included the senate president's own.

After several trips to Iran, I did get to meet the shah. He was very charming. Our firm went on to do some work on the Intercontinental Hotel, but nothing else happened in Iran and we hardly got paid for the hotel work. However, I was able to secure a dozen seats for my employees on a Pan Am plane out of Tehran at a moment when Americans needed desperately to get out, during the fall of the shah and the takeover of the U.S. Embassy there in 1979.

## Wynn Some

A major non-Rockefeller project, while we were under the Rockefeller umbrella, was a casino hotel for entrepreneur Steve Wynn.

One day in my office, I received a phone call from a private airplane—an unusual occurrence in the mid-1970s. The caller was Roger Pelton, a structural engineer from the West Coast whom I knew well. He was calling from Steve Wynn's private plane as they winged eastward from Las Vegas to Atlantic City. Shortly, Roger turned the phone over to Wynn, who explained to me that he had taken over a small Las Vegas casino, the Golden Nugget, and was going to build a much larger one with the same name in Atlantic City. They were still in the design phase for that Atlantic City project, and Roger had argued—as I would have—that this was the time to bring in an experienced construction firm such as Tishman. Wynn asked if I would meet him in Atlantic City when his plane arrived—in two hours.

I said I couldn't do that, but that I would be glad to come to see him there the following morning.

"You're not very interested," Wynn needled.

I demurred; I had other appointments that afternoon but would be there early the next day, with my top executive Milt Gerstman—the man who had been our executive in direct charge of the World Trade Center construction.

Next day, Milt and I met Steve Wynn and Roger Pelton at Steve's new home in Atlantic City. It was undergoing a renovation, the installation of a new office. The men doing the renovation wore Morse/Diesel helmets. What Wynn had not told me, and what Roger may not have known while he had been on the plane, was that Wynn had previously selected our competitor Morse/Diesel to put up his new hotel, and as a favor to him, Morse/Diesel was doing this small alteration. But I learned that Steve hadn't yet signed a contract with Morse/Diesel.

Indicating the workmen, I asked Steve, "Can we talk without these fellows being in the room?"

He agreed, and the four of us went into another room. Steve was impressed with Milt Gershman's role as our lead man on the World Trade Center. As I gave my spiel, I could see that Steve also quite

*Our first project for Steve Wynn, the Golden Nugget in Atlantic City.*

quickly caught on to the idea of Construction Management as the way to work on his hotel. Morse/Diesel had insisted on a cost-plus arrangement, and I stressed how such arrangements could get out of hand due to rising costs, whereas under our concept our firm would work together with him to contain costs. After about a half hour, Steve became restless. He reached over the table and told me that he was going to award us the contract to build his Golden Nugget.

It was an auspicious beginning. I soon got to know, to like, and to greatly admire Steve Wynn. I enjoy people who have a sense of design and who delight in it. Steve is one of those, passionately interested in the esthetics of a building, particularly color. During meetings, he often doodles with colored Magic Markers. It is more than ironic then, that by the time I met him he had already begun to experience the severe vision problems associated with retinitis pigmentosis, a narrowing of the visual field. Steve can be difficult, very demanding of attention, and is very sure of what he wants—but, I have found, those are character-istics shared by all of the best and most successful CEOs. What Steve brings to his enterprises is energy, intelligence, and a willingness to go beyond the ordinary and to reach to make something spectacularly unique.

Steve had begun his gambling business career as a very young man, working the casino tables. His father, who owned a string of bingo parlors in Maryland, died while Steve was still in college, and Steve took over the business. From its profits, he bought a share of the Frontier Hotel and Casino in Las Vegas, and with those profits, and the proceeds of a wine and liquor company that he also owned, he had acquired a controlling interest in the Golden Nugget in Las Vegas.

Along the way, he had also made a friend of Michael Milken, then the leader of the west coast section of Drexel Burnham, a Wall Street brokerage house. Drexel, at Milken's urging, was going to loan Steve quite a bit of money toward the creation of the Atlantic City Golden Nugget—the first time that a Wall Street entity had underwritten any-thing for a gambling-based enterprise.

I knew more than I let on to Steve about Drexel Burnham's part in the operation, as a cousin-in-law of mine was then the company's chairman. The loan to Steve had been approved at a level beneath my cousin-in-law, and as things turned out, I never needed to mention to him that we were going to be working on the project. The deal turned out well for everyone.

Steve put his younger brother in charge of the day-to-day oversight of our work, tutored by Milt Gerstman, who took him under his wing in an almost father-son relationship.

### *Steve, Frank, George, and Donald, Too*

Frank Sinatra from time to time would stay in Mount Kisco, New York with former Mayor Robert F. Wagner, Jr. and his wife Phyllis, neighbors of mine who had become friends, and in whose company I had dined with Old Blue Eyes. I told this to Steve Wynn at one point, and he expressed an interest in meeting Sinatra. I was able to set that up, and Sinatra eventually did a series of promotional ads for Wynn's casinos.

Wynn likes his jokes, and one of the best ones he played on me. I was in Las Vegas, having breakfast with his brother who was in charge of the construction, and his brother Ken informed me that Steve wanted me to meet him on his private golf course. I'm not a golfer, so I wasn't quite sure what he wanted, but when a client asks for a meeting, I'm inclined to respond. So I went out to the golf course, where Steve's associates pointed me out to him, playing on the third hole with a partner that I could not identify from afar. However, there seemed to be a lot of extra security people around, so I became a little bit suspicious. As I walked onto the green to meet Steve, his partner turned around. It was President George H. W. Bush.

"George," Steve said, "I'd like you to meet my carpenter."

And we all had a good laugh.

A laugh of a different sort came about because of the intense competition between Steve Wynn and his rival in the Atlantic City casino business, Donald Trump.

We had never worked for Trump, but one day my office received a call from the Trump Organization summoning me to his office to discuss a project. Since his Fifth Avenue office in The Trump Tower is just a couple of blocks from my office, I walked over, and was soon in a meeting with Donald's brother Robert.

The Trumps knew that we were constructing the Golden Nugget in Atlantic City for Steve Wynn, and wanted to know how much their rival was paying us. I wouldn't divulge that, but I told Robert how we went about Construction Management and what our fees ran between 2 and 5 percent of construction costs. Donald was not in the room but he was in an adjoining one as Robert and I negotiated. He offered us the job of being Construction Manager on the Trump casinos at the same 3¼ percent that we were charging Steve Wynn, and we shook hands on it.

Donald then came into the room. He must have been listening through the walls. He proceeded to try mightily to convince me that taking the Trump job would be good for my firm—that it would "put us on the map" to be associated with the Trump brand.

I responded that we'd been in business since 1898, had constructed hundreds of buildings, had a very solid Construction Management business that had included supervising construction of the World Trade Center towers, and that we didn't need his business to "make" us.

I walked back toward my office, a matter of a few blocks, and by the time I arrived on the 38th floor, my secretary signaled me that Steve Wynn was on the line and that he seemed to be not happy.

"What's this I hear about you working for Trump for 1 percent when you're charging me 3¼ ?!?!?"

In the brief interval between my leaving Trump Tower and reaching my office, it seems, Donald Trump had phoned to needle his rival with the information that he had stolen away Steve's Construction Manager for less money than Steve was paying.

I told Steve the whole story and calmed him down—a bit. But he insisted that I fly to Las Vegas that very night and spend the weekend with him there, so that I could tell the whole Trump story again, in person.

## A Chance at a Hotel

By two years in, under the Rockefeller umbrella, we were managing a billion dollars a year worth of construction for various clients. Only a small percentage of that money stayed in our coffers as fees, but a small percentage of a billion equals millions of dollars, so we were doing very well for the Rockefeller Center Corporation—on schedule to pay off our purchase price within the three years I had initially envisioned for that to happen.

Our burgeoning experience of construction of all types of buildings, including hotels, and our increasingly good relationship with the Disney organization emboldened me to ask Disney whether we could build a new hotel in the part of Disney World known as the hotel strip—not for another owner, but for my division. They were relying on us quite a bit, since, as I've mentioned, many of their construction personnel and executives were busy in Japan, building another Disney World. So when I proposed that our company be considered to build and own a hotel on Disney property, the Disney people fairly quickly said yes, and started to draw up a contract for us to lease land on their hotel strip.

I had already begun to line up the financing for that hotel. Harry Gray, chairman of United Technologies, was a close business friend. UT's divisions included Otis elevators and Carrier air conditioners, and we regularly purchased huge quantities of their products for use in our various construction projects. Moreover, Tishman Research had done joint projects with the UT research laboratories. Harry told me that he would try to arrange for pension funds, including UT's own, to help finance the long-term debt. Since the UT pension fund was administered separately from the UT company, it may have been a bit of a reach for him to assume that the pension fund would go along with him—but not that much of a reach, as Harry was quite confident that this deal would make money for the pension fund. He was frequently quite generous in complimenting me for what our companies did together, which meant a lot to me.

Although the development of a hotel would be a significant leap for us into a new field, development, the prospect was not particularly daunting because of my long experience in the public company, where I had been privy to and part of the decision-making process of developing many other commercial real estate projects. I felt that I knew enough about the development side of the business, and that in erecting a hotel within the fast-expanding Disney World, we would be taking a very reasonable risk. I was also smart enough to recognize that the project—and our company's sanity—would be better off if, after construction was completed, we handed off the day-to-day management of the hotel to a hotel operator such as Hilton, with its gigantic customer base and reservation system. With all these elements in hand—development expertise, financing, and a potential operator for the hotel—and believing that this was a great opportunity, I approached the Rockefeller Center Corporation with the project.

They blinked.

## *Buying the Company—*
## *"With a Little Help From My Friends"*

When seminal events occur, often the cause is not one single thing but a concatenation of several. The Rockefeller Center Corporation was leery of its Tishman division getting into development—because development as a matter of course carried with it substantial risk. At the same time as I proposed this new hotel, change was occurring inside the Rockefeller family as a result of the fourth-generation cousins having doubts about the direction of the various enterprises. Some cousins were environmentalists who didn't like the idea of constructing anything new, especially in big cities, where most of our jobs took us. Others didn't like the idea of any risk-taking, whether done by Cushman & Wakefield, Tishman Construction, or any of the wholly owned Rockefeller entities. Still others wanted to take more money out of the family coffers for themselves, and were pushing for the divestiture of certain "non-core" assets such as the Cushman brokerage and the Tishman construction division.

On my side of the fence, I was ready to have Tishman Construction operate independently, and to own it. Three years earlier that had not been a possibility, so I hadn't really considered it then. But by 1979, since the division was now owned by a private company, Rockefeller, and not by the public Tishman company, it was a good time for me to buy it, and I wanted to. Moreover, while in 1976-77 the real estate market, especially in New York City, had been quite horrific, by 1979 things had turned around and it was booming. Many developers wanted our Construction Management services—a half-dozen large projects awaited us in Manhattan alone, among them the 520 Madison Avenue building that would be the headquarters for Bob and Jerry's firm. And I very much wanted to build and own that hotel at Disney World, something that I could not do without permission from the Rockefeller Center Group so long as our construction division continued under its umbrella. I had asked Rockefeller for permission for my division to have an ownership interest in this project and expressed my willingness for the division to assume the risk position for this opportunity. That last suggestions may have been the straw that broke the camel's back.

Out of a combination of the Rockefeller Group's unwillingness to be involved in the Disney Hilton hotel real estate deal, and Rockefeller wanting to reduce its construction identity, and my eagerness to buy the company, a deal was struck. The Tishman Construction division of the Rockefeller Center Corporation would be sold to me and a group of eighteen of my top executives. The old, public real estate company was now long gone, and as we purchased ourselves from the Rockefeller Center Corporation, we would essentially be undergoing a new birth— as an independent Construction Management firm. In a sense, we were starting a wholly new tradition that encompassed and surpassed the old one. In the new company, my colleagues would receive shares but they would not need to put up any money to buy the company nor would they need to take on any of the risk—I was personally going to assume all of the risk and would arrange for all of the financing.

But I didn't have on hand the $6.5 million that Rockefeller Center and I agreed on as the purchase price. So they assented to my paying for the purchase, in part, out of the proceeds of our operations in the coming years. They knew how well we were doing, and that this repayment shouldn't take very long. But Al Marshall and the other Rockefeller executives needed to have some guarantees that money would continue to come in to the Tishman division, so that they could justify to the Rockefeller family interests the proposed sale of the construction division.

This possibility of buying the company was an opportunity that I could not allow to get away from me.

At that point, as the Beatles song said, I needed "a little help from my friends." We had two major clients, Disney and Steve Wynn, for whom we were working on big projects. I was on good terms with them, which meant that I could discuss my business dealings with them as friends and colleagues. They responded as friends. While I was walking with Steve Wynn in downtown Las Vegas, telling him about my plans for buying the company and my predicament, he—unbidden by me—said, "I'll back you." He offered to assure The Rockefeller Center Corporation that should I not come up with the money to pay them for purchasing the Tishman division, he would hold the $1 million fee to which he was committed for our work, for their benefit. Though he would not put this in writing, he said, he was willing to accept a phone call from a Rockefeller Center executive and to assure him of this commitment.

This was absolutely wonderful, and a testament to the strong working relationship and friendship Steve and I had established. It was a measure of trust—to my mind, the most valuable asset anyone can have.

The top Disney executives also agreed to the same sort of arrangement—to pledge that Disney would hold our next $6 million in fees in abeyance, and pay that directly to Rockefeller, should the need arise.

None of this was put in writing. I did tell the Rockefeller Group executives that Wynn and the Disney top real estate people said that they were willing to accept phone calls on the subject, and then sat back and waited for word that such phone calls had been made.

The phone calls were never placed. It was enough for the Rockefeller honchos to believe my assurance that my largest clients were willing to go that far to back me. In our business, our word is our bond, and the Rockefeller executives, who were also professionals in the real estate field, understood the full implications of the oral pledges given.

Shortly, we finalized the sale of Tishman Construction to me and those construction division executives whom I invited to be limited partners. On February 1, 1980, we began doing business as an independent partnership under my direction. At that time we had more than 350 employees and were handling more than a billion dollars annually in construction projects.

I was thrilled, invigorated, and not much worried about the risks that come with real estate development—except for occasionally late at night, when I would worry a bit.

The transition from the old public company was now complete. We were independent and private—and we had never left home. We still occupied the same offices, at 666 Fifth Avenue, and our major clients were as they had been. Moreover, in the years to come, The Rockefeller Center Corporation continued to utilize our Construction Management services just as often as they had in the past, and just as though we were still a part of their enterprise—an affirmation that the Rockefeller real estate people were still high on us and our services.

Steve Wynn and the Disney folks never had to make good on their verbal pledges to back up our purchase agreement. We were able to fully pay for the purchase of the company from our income within three years of our emancipation.

Now we were really on our own.

# FIVE

# The Disney Experience

## "Mr. Ford Is on the Line"

The first time that my secretary said to me, "Mr. Henry Ford is on the line," I think neither she nor I believed it. But he was, and Ford and I soon hit it off and developed a close relationship. The son of the company's founder was a warm man who answered his own phone and made his own calls. This was in the mid-1970s, when we were still a part of the Tishman public company; Henry Ford, Jr. hired our construction division to help in the planning and supervise the building of the Renaissance Center in Detroit. It was to ultimately feature seven interconnected buildings along the Detroit waterfront, including a 73-story hotel that was to be the world's tallest concrete structure and that today remains the Western Hemisphere's tallest hotel. Famed architect John Portman designed the hotel and the office buildings encircling it. "RenCen" was intended as a "city within a city" in the manner of Rockefeller Center, and its goal was to revitalize downtown Detroit.

For this project Mr. Ford headed a consortium of automobile manufacturers that included Chrysler and General Motors as well as Ford. RenCen was a big project, if not as tall as the 100-story Hancock Center or as large as the World Trade Center towers, which we had already

*Renaissance Center in Detroit, on which we worked with Henry Ford,*
*Jr. and architect John Portman.*

completed. We worked smoothly with the Portman office. Henry Ford attended many of the meetings, absorbed in and contributing to, much of the design and the details of the project. As the reader will recall, it was on RenCen that we condensed the prior ninety-seven steps to making a bathroom, by means of utilizing prefab modules and by arrangements made ahead of installation with the various trades unions. It was our ability to recommend and to carry out such helpful innovations that Mr. Ford said he admired.

There was one glitch, and it was of the sort that frequently arose when we dealt with the boss directly rather than through a client company's in-house project manager. One man in the Ford construction division, a third-tier guy in the overall company hierarchy, became annoyed over time because I was speaking directly to Henry Ford rather than routing all of my queries and responses through him. We at Tishman tried all sorts of ways to compromise with this man and to ease his fears, but none of the strategies worked, and eventually I had to ask Mr. Ford to have him transferred to some other project, since he was getting in the way of completing this one. The man was transferred out, and RenCen was then completed to our client's satisfaction. This glitch taught me a good deal about egos and the sort of turf wars within large corporations that often arise during the constructing of major projects for those corporations.

We have learned to take care not to act in such a manner as to make in-house construction personnel feel that we are competing with them rather than, as we seek to be, working side by side with them. I always want to be able to deal directly with the top man, but I also recognize that to complete the project successfully I need the cooperation of those who report to him or who may be on a lower level.

## The "Imagineers" Tour RenCen

Our reputation for doing big projects attracted the attention of the executives and "imagineers" at The Disney Company. Disneyland in

California was a very successful enterprise, as was the first section of the much larger Disney World in Florida. Before Walt Disney died in 1966, he had made preliminary plans for a sprawling, 600-acre complex adjacent to Disney World in Orlando, to be called EPCOT, for Experimental Prototype Community Of Tomorrow. Two-and-a-half miles from Disney's Magic Kingdom, it was to be more like a self-contained world exposition than a theme park, with many pavilions and showcasing the latest technologies.

I knew from published industry reports that during the construction of the first section of Disney World, the Disney Company had had a bad experience with their general contractor. They had fired the contractor and ended up forming Disney's own construction division and then having their in-house construction people supervise the contractors and subcontractors.

For this next phase, to select a construction firm for EPCOT, the Disney executives decided to go about the task in a different way—in fact, in what I considered the correct way. Rather than simply choose one contractor over another, they did their homework and decided that they would be able to choose among four different approaches to construction supervision. One would be to hire a large General Contractor on a cost-plus basis. A second would be to employ an architectural firm whose project management arm would act as a GC on a cost-plus basis. A third approach would be to use an estimating firm to keep track of the costs incurred by one or more General Contractors. The fourth approach would be to hire a Construction Management firm such as ours, which for a fixed fee—not a cost-plus fee, but a fixed fee—would oversee the work of multiple General Contractors. That they were even considering the Construction Management option spoke well of the Disney executives' knowledge of the business and the challenges facing them in estimating, scheduling, and constructing such a large and multifaceted project.

In any event, four top Disney executives asked to come and see us at work, to inspect something currently under construction, and we made an appointment for them to visit the half-completed Renaissance Center site. The Disney executives arrived, four strong, and wanted to climb all over the construction project, go up ladders, travel on hoists, get their feet dirty, wear construction helmets—the whole nine yards. Ordinarily, I believe that people who want to do this don't fully appreciate how construction works, nor do they understand what questions to ask—and where to ask them—to come out of the process with a recommendation to either use us or a competitor. The real place to obtain the information on which to base such a decision is in our offices, not at a building site where all you can see is motion and half-completed tasks, activities that to my mind are irrelevant to the information that a developer required to come to the basic decision about what sort of construction process to use.

But in this instance, what the Disney executives were doing in traipsing all over this construction site was true due diligence, so that they could report back to their colleagues that they'd seen us in action.

After their tour of the RenCen construction site, the Disney people came to our on-site field office for a demonstration keyed to what I feel to be the most important part of construction, the scheduling program. We were extremely proud of our sophisticated scheduling program, which we had developed in-house for the World Trade Center; it involved the timing of the arrival of materials and precisely when, where, and how the materials were to be put to use. We had done another, similar "CPM"—construction program management—schedule for Renaissance Center, and I envisioned doing the same for the Disney project.

One of our employees had a lot of expertise in the CPM program since he had helped to create it. We had arranged that he would give the presentation, in a room in which the multiple charts and schedules of the RenCen CPM had been pinned to all four walls. He chose to sit on a stool in the center and point to the mounted schedules while he narrated the Construction Management story. During the period when our WTC-veteran executives took the visiting Disney executives and myself on an exhaustive site tour, this man anxiously waited for us all day in the on-site office. The day was inordinately hot, and by the time we all arrived in that room, everyone was sweaty, thirsty, and impatient.

The young man tried to begin the presentation but felt such pressure from the situation that he immediately fainted. He was taken to a couch to revive, and the Disney executives decided to forgo the presentation because they really were more interested, after a hot day and long site tour, in information on where in Detroit to go for good drink, dinner, and entertainment. That, we readily provided.

Shortly thereafter, I convinced the Disney executives that what they wanted was not a General Contractor but Tishman Construction as their Construction Manager. I explained how they would, in effect, rent our construction company, and that we would work directly for them as a part of their team. This arrangement would allow the two firms to jointly control costs and adhere to schedules. We would add our "owner/builder" input to the design process, supervise the bidding process, and do everything else associated with managing the construction for a fixed fee that would be a percentage of the overall construction budget. They liked the idea. As a Disney executive later told the *Engineering News-Record*, they were impressed by more than our track record: "There was … a certain flexibility in [Tishman's] approach that left us with a gut feeling that these people would be able to adapt to our way of doing things, that the two organizations would interact well."

We were hired—and then, as discussed in the previous chapter, the project was shelved for a while, due to the Middle East War, the oil embargo, and the subsequent economic downturn.

I was very favorably impressed by the Disney style, their belief in quality control, and their company consciousness. No matter what level the executives were on, from the construction honchos to the top management, they seemed to have very little personal ego involved in what they were doing; it was all about being proud to be part of Disney. Several times, while walking around the Disney parks, I saw a top executive bend down and pick up a stray piece of trash in just as natural a manner as if he had been on his own front lawn or if he had been a designated groundskeeper rather than an executive, and without calling attention to the task or to himself for doing it. Working with the Disney people, I concluded, was going to be a pleasure.

While EPCOT was on hold, the Disney people put us to work on a second-phase addition to their Polynesian hotel. This was a relatively small, $8 million project, but I knew that it was a test to see whether we were really going to be able to handle the then-$800 million EPCOT project. So I assigned Milt Gerstman, the lead man on the WTC project, to the Polynesian, even though someone less senior could have supervised it. We completed the building in late May on a schedule that had called for us doing so by June, and only then found out that Disney had expected completion for occupancy in August. We also completed our objective: to meet and pass their test. Now we could build EPCOT—and the first hotel under our ownership.

Construction of the Disney Polynesian was done during the period when we were operating under Rockefeller ownership and before we went out on our own in 1980, having won the right to construct our own hotel on Disney property. It was to be an 814-room hotel, timed to open when EPCOT did. That eventually happened, but not easily—and thereby hang several tales.

## Building EPCOT

First, the tale of EPCOT itself. Disney's Experimental Prototype Community of Tomorrow was actually a larger construction project than the World Trade Center had been in terms of the amount of area covered, the number of buildings—each one distinct—and the complexity of all the elements. Each main building was to be known as a pavilion, and there would be twenty pavilions, plus associated support structures and infrastructure, and an enclosed lagoon. The whole would cover some 600 acres, which was to be carved out of very swampy land, including some large sinkholes, that teemed with alligators, snakes, and other critters in the muck and mire. Each pavilion was to appear physically very different from the other nineteen, and many of them were to be quite intricate and unusual, containing such machinery as moving platforms, as well as theaters, restaurant facilities, carnival-type rides, and the largest aquarium in the world.

The way that the Disney Company worked, its "Imagineers" first created the basic design for each pavilion, sort of impressionistic sketches for freestanding sculptures and their surrounding environments. Then these sketches were turned over to outside architectural firms that would complete the actual working drawings and details that construction teams could execute. They awarded the design for each pavilion to a different architect. Although the work was lucrative for the architects, the chosen firms had to sign very restrictive contracts: they were not permitted to claim—ever—that they had designed the pavilion, or to use a photograph or a representation of their work on it in any of their brochures or advertising. For us, this Disney design system meant that for each pavilion in EPCOT, we had to deal with separate architectural and engineering firms.

Monthly, I flew to Disney headquarters in California to brief top Disney executives and members of their board on the progress of EPCOT, as I had begun to do with the Polynesian. The attention of the top executives to every detail of the construction and its scheduling was extremely high.

Our production schedules were at the heart of our work for Disney on EPCOT. Such schedules are the guts of any Construction Management job; everything flows from them—the final revisions of drawings, the assembling of bid packages for the multiple contractors and materials, and the development of strategies for contracting, purchasing, and staffing. For EPCOT's schedules, we began by making up a preliminary milestone chart that showed, to us and to Disney, the scope of the job in broad strokes. Then we broke that chart down into smaller sections, each with its own chart. Eventually we produced hundreds of schedules interrelating about 2,000 different activities.

The method of scheduling was the same as for the World Trade Center towers, but while during the WTC project the logistics had a vertical axis, at EPCOT the need was to plan the logistics on a horizontal axis. In turns, this meant such things as having to plan for and carve out parking lots for the construction workers' cars, some 2,500 of them each day. We had to create those lots, and a lagoon (where there had not been one) and a major monorail system, as well as major access roads leading to and from EPCOT to the nearby highways—and all of this had to be done before any pavilions could be erected.

## Future World

There were to be two parts to EPCOT, Future World and World Showcase.

Future World was to be a circular area containing six large pavilions, each with a different theme—"energy," "communications," "the seas"—and all of them arranged around a spectacular center, a 165-foot diameter geodesic sphere of shiny aluminum known as Spaceship Earth. Visible from miles away, it was the symbol of the entire EPCOT complex. Wags referred to it as the Golf Ball.

Disney wanted to have each Future World pavilion sponsored by a major industrial firm. AT&T, Kodak, Exxon, Kraft Foods, and General Electric became involved, Exxon, for instance, in the pavilion devoted to energy. In that pavilion, visitors would view a show displayed on huge screens and dioramas while they were transported in moving sleds on a conveyor belt. AT&T was to provide the show that was inside the central geodesic dome, a multifaceted look at the progress of human communications from the caveman era to the present day.

*Our largest project in terms of land area, number of buildings,
and complexity: EPCOT at Disney World.*

A third pavilion, whose theme was the oceans, was to contain the world's largest aquarium; its visitors could walk right alongside the aquarium and sometimes through the parts.

I had the ideal candidate to underwrite that aquarium, United Technologies. Harry Gray was interested, and with his blessing and the permission of the Disney board, I presented the case for this $50 million project to the board of United Technologies. The UT board liked the idea and signed on. Some of their products, including Otis elevators, were to be used in this pavilion and in several others. The elevator in this big-aquarium pavilion was going to shake and shiver, to give visitors the impression that they were descending several hundred feet to the level of the sea bottom, although the elevator would travel only a few feet down.

The aquarium was a marvel. Huge, it was also compartmentalized so that it could be stocked with over 1,500 varieties of fish and marine life. Every space in the pavilion was to face the aquarium, so that, for instance, diners in the restaurant could have a full view of the living backdrop as they ate their meals.

Construction of the aquarium was quite complicated. Water is very heavy, and large volumes of it exert substantial pressure, more and more of it as you go down toward the bottom. Because of the immense water pressure, near the bottom portion of the aquarium the viewing glass had to be nine inches thick, although the glass in each window was to become thinner as it went upward, to the point where at the top it would only be one inch thick. The thickest glass had to be imported from Japan, the only place of manufacture. It was a manufacturing challenge to maintain strength and transparency without distortion through this thickness of glass.

Every Future World pavilion presented similar challenges. The pavilion devoted to invention had a theater in which the seats were to move, jiggle, and tickle patrons with air jets; the machinery and the structure to support it were quite complex. The people-movers and other contraptions in the pavilions rivaled those of NASA's astronaut-training machinery. One of them, for which visitors had to be strapped into their seats with belts across chests, laps, and legs, made them feel as though they were in hang gliders, soaring over the landscape.

Disney wrote ten-year leases for sponsoring the Future World pavilions; during that period of time, the big companies were permitted to have stores in the pavilions to promote their products. Each pavilion also came with a VIP area equipped for use for corporate and board meetings. After the ten years concluded, the companies were to relinquish the pavilions to Disney, which could then renew or replace the sponsors.

## World Showcase

The second part of EPCOT, called World Showcase, was to contain eleven pavilions, grouped so as to surround a large lagoon. These pavilions were to be devoted to individual countries—the U.S., Canada, United Kingdom, France, Italy, Germany, China, Japan, Mexico, Norway, and Morocco. Each pavilion was designed to display the distinctive architectural look of its country. Inside, there were to be attractions, rides, big-screen presentations, and the like, as well as shops selling souvenirs and foods characteristic of each country.

"This place is a jungle," said more than one of my construction executives to me during the three years of building EPCOT. Actually, the place was not a jungle but a swamp, akin to the nearby Everglades. Florida panthers, alligators, rattlesnakes and other poisonous pests roamed the site. But the biggest problem was the ground—or, I should say, the lack of solid ground.

Smack in the center of the 600 acres was a huge sinkhole. Sinkholes are geological formations that can be as old as 15 million to 25 million years. This one had been waiting for us quite a while, and its boundaries were not fixed—regularly, cars and trucks that we thought had been on safe solid ground would start to sink in and would have to be rescued by a tow-truck. The sinkhole was full of organic silt and peat, and the sand underneath went down as far as 300 feet. Nothing solid could be built on it, since the underlying sand could not support the weight of a building. The most logical thing to do with the largest sinkhole of all was to dig it deeper and make it into the lagoon around which the World Showcase pavilions would be situated.

Simple idea, difficult thing to do. Under our direction, three general contractors specializing in heavy construction worked on the area. First, they had to construct a bathtub containing an area that could be filled with enough water in which to float a dredge to excavate and remove the muck. The muck was five feet thick and there was a million cubic yards of it to be removed so that the underlying sand could properly serve as the lagoon bottom. Complicating the task of removal were two huge "root islands" in the muck. Unable to get them out, we eventually poured onto them a half-million yards of sand taken from another part of the lagoon. Then, top-heavy with sand, the root islands sank beneath the surface of the water and stayed there. Today, looking at the lagoon, you see no evidence of them. But they are there, beneath the surface, and the boats that ply the lagoon know to avoid them.

The various country pavilions of World Showcase around the lagoon were each to sit on a wedge-shaped piece of property. The U.S. pavilion would be the largest, and it took up two wedges. Moreover, it was located along the North-South line, directly opposite to Future World's Spaceship Earth, the sphere-shaped emblem of EPCOT. Disney suggested that each country obtain funding for its pavilion from a major industry within the country, e.g., Germany, from its beer industry. Each pavilion could have a shop selling that country's merchandise, but with a catch: the merchandise, ranging from small souvenirs to larger-ticket luxury goods, had to be selected by Disney's own shoppers. Each pavilion would also offer some of that country's characteristic foods—prepared solely by Disney in their immense central kitchens.

Design and construction of EPCOT was done on a crash basis—in three years, a very rapid timetable for so sprawling a project. For various reasons, including favorable tax benefits and to catch the beginning of the winter tourist season, EPCOT needed to open before September 30, 1982.

We were determined to make that deadline, and to do so integrated our firm with Disney's in every way possible. For instance, we moved one of our executives from Chicago to an office at Disney in California to work on the pre-construction documents and to critique the designs in terms of the practicality and cost of the construction. For another instance, Disney had envisioned a 195-foot diameter sphere for the Spaceship Earth; we recommended downsizing it to a 165-foot diameter because the larger sphere would have been much more expensive than the smaller one but it would not have provided any additional exhibit or ride space.

After the critical pre-construction phase, the action moved to the site. The keys to completing any large and complex task on time and on budget are planning and a good computer scheduling system. The construction of EPCOT took place during an era when computers were not as agile as they are today, but we used the best computers we could find. We also required each contractor to do the same, to use "critical path" planning of the sort that we had evolved for the WTC projects; we called ours T-COM. The project involved numerous general contractors, and these had even more numerous subcontractors, sub-subs, and suppliers. We insisted that all the GCs provide us first with milestone schedules and then with detailed fieldwork schedules, and, while in construction, to update the field schedules every sixty days. To provide us with these schedules, they had to obtain precise and regular input from their subs. All the data accumulated through these contractors were fed into the computer, and the results provided to our 200 CM people on-site. Construction took approximately 1,000 days, and each day was jam-packed with tasks to be done. After all, we were creating from scratch a sprawling city to which an average of 30,000 people would come, each day—and they would be there to be entertained, fed, and transported.

In addition to building the pavilions, we built the monorail system that ties EPCOT to the other parts of Disney World, such as Magic Kingdom. The monorail was to be made of pre-cast concrete sections; since the only plant that could do the work was in Oregon, and the cross-country transport costs would be too great, so we even built a pre-casting factory on site to make the a variety of structural sections. Eventually, we ended up building parts of Magic Kingdom, too.

## A Hotel at Disney World

During the period when we were completing Disney's Polynesian Hotel, and when the top Disney construction executives were still engaged in building the Disney World in Japan, the need for additional hotels in Florida came up at a Disney board meeting. They determined a need for a hotel on a particular piece of property adjacent to other hotels on the strip just outside Disney World—today, the location of Walt Disney World Village, a small city referred to in the Orlando area as "downtown Disney."

"What about us?" I fearlessly asked the Disney board. I had no hesitation in doing so because I'd been working as an owner/builder for more than thirty years and had done all sorts of commercial construction. I hoped that the Rockefeller Group would permit me to do such a project, but I knew that even if they didn't, this was too good an opportunity to pass up. To be permitted to build a hotel that Disney wanted, on a prime piece of property within Disney World, and with the knowledge that EPCOT would soon be constructed and bring additional visitors to the site—now there was a recipe for success!

Without much ado, the Disney board approved the idea of Tishman constructing a hotel for its own ownership. The board had become dissatisfied with some of the existing hotel owners and operators in the Village, and wanted a hotel built—and maintained and operated— up to their standards of quality control, and they already knew how well we worked and operated. Harry Gray helped us to obtain interim financing we needed through his Hartford friends at the Travelers and Aetna insurance companies.

By the time the deal to construct the hotel was completed, we had left the Rockefeller fold and had gone out on our own. With this hotel, and our independence, we had come full circle, re-entering the ranks of owner-builders while continuing our Construction Management business.

This was our first hotel, and despite my fearlessness in asking for the opportunity to build and own it, a hotel was a big risk for us. Hotels usually take five or more years to begin to pay a good return on investment, whereas office towers can be profitable as soon as they are rented. But I understood the risk on this hotel and was willing to bear it—after all, the hotel would be within Disney World and therefore would be likely to have sufficient occupancy and a high enough room rate, the keys to hotel profitability.

Construction proceeded without incident—in fact, very quickly, in just sixteen months—and our 814-room hotel opened in 1984. We selected Hilton to run it because of their worldwide reservation system and reputation. Having Hilton run the hotel worked better than if we had directly supervised the hotel's day-to-day operations. We continued to own and asset-manage the property and to be involved with Hilton in all important decisions regarding key personnel, operating procedures, and the sort of periodic renovations that keep hotels up to date and attractive to customers.

Shortly after we began to construct this hotel, the opportunity arose for doing something even larger at the Disney property—the first on-site hotel to be designed as a convention center. In the early days of conceptualizing the theme parks, Walt Disney and his colleagues did not envision their Disneyland and Disney World attractions as being anything more than tourist and leisure destinations, but as time went on the notion of having convention center facilities available on site at Disney World became more alluring. While Mr. John Q. Executive attended a convention of, say, insurance underwriters at the convention hall during business hours, Mrs. Mary Executive and the couple's children could be enjoying themselves at the Disney World theme parks, a possibility that could turn a business trip into a family vacation—with lots more money to be made by the Disney Company.

I was in the process of delivering one of my monthly reports to the Disney executives and board members in California when the discussion turned to the need for a convention center hotel. "What about us?" I again asked. Since we were already building the Hilton and had completed their Polynesian renovation, we were a logical, available, and trusted source.

The immediate answer was yes.

I jumped at the chance. But I insisted on inserting into the contract for the convention center hotel a clause specifying that Disney must not build (or allow others to build) a larger convention center facility in the area for ten years after ours opened. This meant that no other hotel would be permitted to have a ballroom larger than 100,000 square feet—ours would be much larger than that. A huge ballroom is the key to accommodating significant numbers of conventioneers in a single place. Another part of the clause said that competing hotels could also not have ancillary facilities such as a high number of meeting rooms.

With a minimum of fuss, the Disney executives signed this contract, and we planned a groundbreaking ceremony. Disney took over the preparations for that ceremony and made it into a grand one, replete with Mickey Mouse leading the festivities, marching bands, and their top executives turning over shovels full of dirt for the benefit of the television cameras. Those executives included two brand new ones, Michael Eisner and Frank Wells—who, that day, were all smiles as they took part in the festivities and examined the detailed, full-scale model of the entire Disney World area, including EPCOT and our proposed hotel.

*Ground-breaking for our first hotel at Disney World. Michael Eisner and Frank Wells had only recently joined the Walt Disney Company.*

## Breakfast with Frank, Lunch with Michael

Between the signing of our contract for the convention center hotel and the ground-breaking in 1984, The Disney Company had fallen into a weakened financial position and two outside buyers had sought to purchase the company, break it up, and sell off its component parts. Roy Disney, Walt's brother, had fought to preserve the company, and in that battle one of his advisors had been Frank Wells. A former vice-chairman of Warner Bros., Wells had been biding his time outside of Hollywood climbing the highest mountains in the world. Wells advised Roy to have the Disney company hire as its CEO Michael Eisner, who in eight years as head of Paramount had produced a string of movie hits ranging from *Saturday Night Fever* to *Terms of Endearment*. Beginning as a page at ABC in 1963, Eisner had worked his way up in television to be head of that company before moving to Paramount. The Disney board was willing to hire Eisner as CEO but only if Wells came along as the financial guru and COO. One of the duo's first accomplishments was to convince a major Disney stockholder, the Bass family, to make a public statement that they would not sell their Disney stock for five years; this helped quell market misgivings about The Disney Company's prognosis for recovery.

Two months after the ground-breaking ceremony for our hotel that Eisner and Wells had attended, and as construction on our hotel was about to begin in earnest, I learned by reading an article in the *Orlando Sentinel* that Disney was planning to build a larger hotel than ours at EPCOT. This was a clear violation of our contract, so I had our lawyer write Disney a letter citing the existing contract and directing them to cease and desist on any plans for a competing convention-center hotel. Eisner and Wells refused, saying that the existing contract was non-binding, for various reasons. Among them (at various times) they asserted that the contract did not have the proper signature on it, or that the person who had signed it for Disney had not had the authority to do so. We showed them that a parent company Disney executive had signed the contract, and that he had had full authority to sign it. They continued to disagree.

Frank Wells phoned to ask if we could have breakfast in New York. I took this overture, in part, as a sign that he and Eisner knew that on this issue their legal position was weak. But I also had to be careful in dealing with Wells, since any future work that we might do for or with Disney could be compromised should we be unable to breach this impasse. We already had financial partners and hotel operators on board. Sheraton and Westin Hotels were going to operate the hotels for us, and our financial partners included Metropolitan Life Insurance and Aoki, a Japanese firm.

Wells and I had breakfast at the Mayflower Hotel. A big, athletic man with a confident and elegant manner, Wells tried to make a rather convoluted "good faith" argument: that a corporation could make an agreement but then change its mind and repudiate it—so long as it did so in good faith. In other words, we must go along with him and Eisner because they were now in charge at Disney and they could repudiate past contracts. As politely as I could, I laughed at him. He smiled as well.

Next, Michael Eisner called and wanted to lunch with me. Of course I said yes. Eisner is quite tall, very forceful, and very charming. He acknowledged the factuality of the agreement that had been signed between Tishman and Disney, but said it had to be scrapped and Disney must build its own convention center, and was going to do so. This was a very polite "Drop dead."

We heard rumors that Disney wanted to bring in Marriott to build the convention center and then to take over all the hotels within Disney World.

I decided that if Disney was going to play rough, I would have to do the same. I immediately halted construction at the hotel site. Then, after apprising my partners, who included Rand Araskog, the legendary chairman of Sheraton (a division of ITT), we sued Disney for breach of contract, for $350 million. That would have been bad enough, but we did so under the RICO Act, a racketeering statute that would allow us to claim triple damages; the value of the entire suit thus became over $1 billion. And we purposefully filed this suit and announced it publicly not far in advance of the annual Disney shareholders meeting.

Eisner later said he didn't mind the dollar amount of the suit, but that he did mind the epithet, being called a racketeer and sued as one. He reacted strongly. He located Rand Araskog at a hotel in Mexico and, even though Eisner had never met Rand, woke him up by telephone at three in the morning to complain about the suit. I later learned that Eisner had also called Met Life, and had a conversation with a top executive there in which he argued that two mega-businesses, Met Life and Disney, must not allow pipsqueaks such as a small, privately owned construction firm to successfully sue them. He wanted Met Life to pressure me to withdraw the suit. Neither Met Life nor Sheraton suggested any such thing to me; they both strongly supported our position.

Unable to crack my coalition, and with the threat of the suit and its attendant bad publicity hanging over him, Eisner called me and strongly suggested that we compromise.

## *The Grand Compromise*

To me, the suit against Disney was a matter of principle. We were in the right, and that was that. Thus in any proposed settlement I had no interest in being monetarily compensated for what we owned. Eisner seemed to understand this and not to attempt to buy us out of our position. He now agreed that by contract we had the right to build the convention center hotel, but he asked that we change both the design and the location— and he said Disney would pay for any overage accompanying those changes. His complaint was that the design of the hotel, done by architect Alan Lapidus, was "plain vanilla," and that such a design did not meet Disney's sense of the theatrical and of what its customers looked for in a Disney-associated facility, particularly since, by contract, we would have the Disney name on the hotel. The hotels would be known as Disney hotels—we would be the only outside firm permitted to use the Disney name in such a way.

All of this made a lot of sense to me. So I kept on listening.

What Eisner wanted was a concept that he and others later labeled "entertainment architecture," buildings that had the Disney flair and style. He also wanted us to build at the far end of the EPCOT lagoon. The site he chose was within EPCOT rather than the property Disney had previously allocated to us, which was just outside its gates. Clearly, to be within EPCOT proper was much more viable in terms of our hotels' future profitability. Eisner envisioned two linked hotels, to be called the Dolphin and the Swan, and he imagined huge statues of a dolphin and a swan, each in its respective hotel's outer courtyard and very visible from inside EPCOT as well as from afar. To design the hotels, Eisner wanted to hire a visionary architect, one whom we were to agree upon mutually. After seeing a couple of presentations, we decided upon Michael Graves, an architect so innovative and well regarded that an even more famous architect, Robert A. M. Stern, had commissioned him to design Stern's own home. Graves accepted, and came up with the Dolphin and Swan themes, eventually represented by huge statues of these animals, each atop one of the hotels, very visible from afar— from within EPCOT as well as outside of it. Alan Lapidus was also rehired for the practical aspects of Graves' new designs.

This was a grand compromise, and one of the best solutions to a very complicated problem in which I'd ever had a part. After our suit was withdrawn and the compromise proposed, the acrimony vanished and everyone cooperated. The results were spectacular, not only in terms of the hotels' attractiveness but in their profitability to us and to Disney, and in their utility to Disney in the servicing of massive conventions by means of ballrooms seating 6,000 in the Dolphin and 2.500 in the Swan.

The "dolphin" and "swan" motifs are carried on throughout the exteriors of the hotels and in the lobbies—clamshell fountains on the Dolphin exterior, a four-swan fountain as the center of the Swan, exterior painting of waves and other water motifs. Water cascades from an upper story of the Dolphin to a dolphin pool below. The entire com-

*After the grand compromise: examining sculptures for the Dolphin and Swan Hotels at EPCOT.*

plex's design elements highlight the idea that this is a place in which the visitor is expected to have fun. Everything is bright, open, clean, and interesting, as well as being functional. Eisner remained fully involved in the minutiae of the design process, putting forth his ideas on such details as the uniforms to be worn by the waitresses in the restaurants. Our design sessions were full of interest, quite engaging for me in many ways, not the least of them the opportunity to develop a working relationship with Eisner, Wells, and Graves. Wells became a good friend outside of the Disney context. We shared the same political and social beliefs, and I admired him for everything he stood for. Frank enjoyed life to the maximum and surprised all of us with his humor at the opening ceremony of EPCOT's Living Seas Pavilion. Out of nowhere, Frank appeared, in full diver gear, descending through the then-largest aquarium in the world, and waving at us through the glass.

I learned a great deal in the financing, the design, and the operating of the Dolphin and Swan. Perhaps the most important lesson was the extent to which hotels are theatrical experiences, mandating that they must be designed and operated with that notion in mind. In a hotel, as opposed to a commercial office building, utility is not everything. People come to Disney World to be entertained, and their hotel experience is part of that feeling. The same has now become true of all our "company-owned" hotels across the country.

## Uncle Paul's African Art Collection

The Disney Imagineers initially gave some thought to having a pan-African pavilion for the World Showcase area. But this presented some problems. For one thing, very few industries in Africa were large enough to sponsor such an endeavor, and those that were, such as the De Beers diamond company, were associated with questions about their business practices. Moreover, the African continent contains many countries and even more cultures, and to highlight one country or culture would be to shortchange the others. During the pre-Eisner era, when a sort of pan-African pavilion was being considered, I suggested to the Disney executives that Disney purchase the largest and most significant collection of African art then in private hands, the one that had been lovingly assembled over several decades by my uncle Paul Tishman.

Paul was getting on in years and as he wound down his operations and shut down his private general contracting firm, my firm had absorbed many of his employees. He needed money for his declining years and for that purpose had determined to sell his well known and highly regarded collection. More important to him than selling it was to have it purchased as an intact collection, even though breaking up the collection and selling the pieces individually might have brought him more money.

Most of the collection was from West and Central Africa, although there were examples from many of the continent's cultures. Outside experts agreed that Paul's collection covered most of the continent's major art styles. It featured masks and figurines, among the latter a 17th century crucifix depicting a Christ with African features, created in the area that later came to be called the Congo during the century after European missionaries had first visited. There was a four-faced helmet mask—a man and three wives—from the Akparabong area of Nigeria, and a copper rooster from Nigeria's Benin area. Other prominent items from the nearly one thousand pieces included an elephant mask from the Guro people of the Ivory Coast, a three-foot high naturalistic male figure from Madagascar that rivaled the similar masterpieces of the ancient Greeks and Romans, a 500-year-old ivory salt-cellar, and a mask from Cameroon whose amber eye-pieces were made from spiders' silk. The oldest and most rare item was a 15th-century hunting horn from Sierra Leone. "This is the collection that scholars in the field have literally grown up with," one expert later remarked.

The Disney executives liked the notion of buying the collection. So did Alex Haley, author of *Roots*, the famed book that became a television series about American blacks rediscovering their African roots. Haley, who had previously been hired as a consultant to Disney, recommended the purchase, and Disney paid Paul $3 million for it. Although this was a considerable amount of money at the time, it paled in comparison with the sale of individual Picassos and of works by other artists; to me, the $3 million price was an indication of how underappreciated African art was at the time. The purchase contract specified that the collection must be kept intact and that individual pieces would not be sold off. Disney hired a curator for the collection, treated the collection well, and attempted to find interesting ways to display it. They finally settled on the idea of a pavilion containing a series of African "huts" that a visitor could walk through, and in which visitors could view the artworks.

While they were mulling over this configuration, Wells and Eisner came aboard, and I proceeded to have with them the same sort of tussle over the African art collection that we'd had over the convention center hotel. They first argued that the "whereas" clauses and other wordings of the contract were not binding and that they could indeed sell off individual pieces of the collection. Eisner did not want an African pavilion or a series of huts, whether or not they contained art; he thought that a pan-African pavilion ought to contain some sort of safari-oriented thrill ride. He argued that because no corporate sponsor could be found, the African huts were not a good business idea for Disney.

In time, Frank Wells came over to my point of view, that the Paul Tishman African art collection was a valuable thing in and of itself and that Disney should continue to own it. Frank became its inside guardian. He would send me handwritten notes when institutions sought to borrow various pieces for exhibitions, as happened frequently. My own sense of stewardship for the collection continued, unabated.

Michael Eisner also came around to accepting that the collection was valuable and should be kept intact, even if it was sold. Later, he told me that he had spoken to President Jacques Chirac about purchasing it when the two were in negotiations for a Disneyland in France;

it would have gone to the Musée de l'Homme, in Paris, the world's leading anthropological museum. That transaction did not take place, but still later, when Eisner was about to leave The Disney Company after more than a decade, one of his final acts was to donate the collection, intact, to the Smithsonian Institution in Washington, where it has become the Disney Tishman African Art Collection, on display for millions of visitors each year. That was a very fitting end to the saga, one that gratified me and would have gratified Paul, who by that time had long since passed on.

## Later On, with Disney

A large part of my working life has been tied to working with the Disney Company on various projects, and I am proud of those projects and of the long association. Building ECPOT and the hotels remains one of my best legacies—it's not every builder who is able to say that more than ten million people a year visit a place that his company has constructed.

Our company continued to build for and with Disney, rather intensely, for a half-dozen years after the completion of EPCOT and the Dolphin and Swan Hotels. By that time, the Disney construction executives had returned from Japan, and decided that they, rather than we, should be overseeing any construction done on Disney properties. I understood this and also sensed that this was a turf war and that a new Disney construction chief did not want us competing for his bosses' ears.

Fortunately we had many other projects to do, and we had a continuing relationship with Disney through our three hotels serving Disney World and EPCOT. Interestingly enough, even after the elapse of the ten-year moratorium period for a convention center, no equal-size convention center hotels were erected in the area, which attests to Disney's satisfaction with the one we had created. We have made sure to uphold our part of the arrangement with Disney by spending liberally to update and refit the hotels over the years.

As the 1990s began, the Disney people called us in on three projects in midtown New York City, two in Times Square, the New Amsterdam Theater and the ESPN store in Times Square; the third project, the studio of WABC, the ABC network's flagship television station, was also in Times Square. On the latter two projects, general contractors had been engaged at the outset but there had been some problems with them. My take on why the contractors had failed was, among other reasons, Disney's proclivity for "designing as you go" in the midst of construction. Our CM approach more easily encompassed this sort of evolving-idea construction.

I contributed a bit to bringing Disney to 42nd Street. One day, several Disney executives and I visited the then-decrepit New Amsterdam Theatre on 42nd Street. Mushrooms were growing in the interior. There

*The New Amsterdam Theater, a beautiful restoration*
*for the Disney Company, in the Times Square area.*

was water all through the building, and the holes in the roof were large enough to see through. Yet the old interior had a grandeur that more recently constructed theaters could not match. An optimist, I assured the Disney executives that this wreck of a theater could be renovated to house the musicals that Disney wanted to bring to Broadway, and that in renovating it and becoming a presence on 42nd Street, Disney could help turn around a section of New York that had once been spectacular but that had fallen very far into the depths. This meshed with Michael Eisner's vision, and the "landmark" New Amsterdam Theater lived again. Revitalizing that end of 42nd Street also enabled our firm and New York City to resuscitate an even larger portion of "the Deuce"— the street name for 42nd.

# Inventing Construction Management

## "Master Builders" and a Bit of History

Tishman Construction is generally recognized as the creator of the field of Construction Management; and the CMAA, the Construction Management Association of America, has honored me as a pioneer. I'm not very good at patting myself on the back, but on this point I must quote the letter from the CMAA that accompanied my award: "Your work in establishing the value of the 'team' in the entire development process, introducing the concepts of fast-track construction and the systems approach to product specification, as well as involving manufacturers/suppliers in finding innovative solutions to building problems has had a tremendous impact on the CM industry."

Construction Management is the innovation of which I am the most proud, in part because of the way I think of Construction Management as the modern equivalent of the old "master builder" concept, which dates to the Greek and Roman eras but reached its apogee in the early Middle Ages. A master builder would make the design and then supervise the construction phases from start to finish, integrating the work of the trades and the suppliers of materials, and controlling the payments to everyone involved. Sometimes this master builder was the owner of the property; more often he worked for an organization such as the church or a governmental entity that needed an edifice erected. In many and varied ways, the master builder acted as the manager and coordinator of all aspects of the project.

In the late Middle Ages, this arrangement changed with the coming to prominence of the profession of architect, and as guilds of tradesmen such as carpenters, plumbers, and masons gained some collective power. Each aspect of creating a building became specialized. The architect created the design but was not responsible for supervising the construction. Each trade operated somewhat independently of the others.

In the nineteenth century, owners and their architects began hiring one manager or one firm to supervise all of the various building trades. They made a contract with this person or firm to act as the "general" contractor, whose task it was to pay for and to supervise the work of the specialized tradesmen.

In the twentieth century, the norm for real estate development, particularly in the big cities, became entrepreneurs with little construction expertise who therefore needed to hire general contractors to erect their buildings. The major exceptions to this norm were Tishman Realty & Construction and similar family-owned developers, who supervised their own construction. By the end of World War II, in New York, only Tishman Realty, of the large New York-based developers, continued to have its own construction division.

## The General Contractor and His Ills

In the 1960s, as I began to supervise large-scale construction for other clients and developers, I believed that for commercial projects, the day of the general contractor was past—and that it had to be over because the model was flawed. To understand why I considered the general contractor model of supervising construction to be outmoded, we need to look more closely at the process of creating a building.

The first step is the decision on whether to build on a particular site. The owner may have held the site for some time, or may only have determined more recently that a new facility is needed or that something should be built as an investment for the owner and/or outside investors.

The second step is for the owner to define the project criteria, such as the total square footage needed and permitted on the site, and to come up with a budget for construction. In some cases, an owner will perform these calculations with his own staff; frequently, though, he brings in outside consultants so that he or she is not guessing on any of the numbers but is making reasonable estimates.

The third step is the delivery, the constructing of the project. This phase has several sub-steps in it, which I'll detail. In the traditional—and, I believe, in the most stilted and archaic—form of project delivery, the design is fully completed before an experienced construction expert is brought on board.

The first part of the delivery process is the bid phase. In it, the owner is faced with two prime alternatives for project completion. One is a competitive-bid procedure in which plans and specs are issued to those general contractors who are interested in building the job, and the contract is then awarded to the lowest bidder. The alternative to the competitive-bid approach is a negotiated contract; the owner negotiates with one or more GCs until they can agree on a guaranteed maximum price or a fixed-price contract.

Unfortunately, both of these configurations place the owner and the GC on opposite sides of the table, where they must negotiate with each other, one way or another. In both configurations, the GC makes its money by controlling its costs. This creates a situation in which the GC is likely to provide the owner with high estimates of the costs of materials and labor in order to cover potential problems during the construction phase, and also to cut corners wherever possible to keep his own costs low and to heighten his profit margin. Because of these likelihoods, maximum-price contracts and fixed-price contracts with GCs do not generally benefit either the owner or the project itself.

Historically, placing the owner and contractor on opposite sides of the table fostered a climate in which bid-rigging became prevalent. All too often, the night before bids were to be delivered to a potential client, the executives of the several large GCs would get together and decide amongst themselves who would be the low bidder and thus merit the contract; the notion was to spread the work around so that each GC would have enough work to be profitable, and not at the expense of one another. In big American cities such as New York, this had been an unofficial arrangement. In Japan, it was close to being an official arrangement. Japan's top industrial firms apportioned all of their work according to a schedule and formula set up by the general contractors themselves.

Design and bidding are pre-construction phases. During the actual construction, additional problems inevitably crop up, and under the GC system, their solutions invariably add costs to the GC's operation that the GC must then renegotiate with the owner. Let's be realistic: over the length of time needed to build a project, it is quite natural that proposed changes in the design will develop. When this happens under the GC system, the owner or architect must enter into new negotiations with the GC to define the scope and cost of the desired changes, and to determine who will pay the extra cost associated with the changes.

This is always the point in the building process where the plot thickens.

What now becomes apparent, if it had not already been so, is that the owner has started the building process at a disadvantage because he is using the general contracting approach. The disadvantages are accelerating as the inevitable design changes crop up. During the before-bid design phase, if the owner had less than adequate construction expertise onboard, he had no good way of evaluating the architect's design in terms of construction costs. From a construction point of view, the designs may have been impractical, but the owner will have been unaware of this because of the dearth of expertise on his side of the table during that phase, and the ramifications of his being inadequately advised will ramp up as the time comes for design changes during actual construction. Then, too, he will be unaware that far less expensive techniques might be available for use than the ones recommended by the architect. Nor will his general contractor have told him that—GC's generally do not suggest alternatives to architects' designs. The owner's lack of construction expertise in the design phase can and often does more than lead to extra costs—it can cause real problems.

The major problem is that costs can do far more than go up a few percent—they can spiral out of control. Since while using a GC the owner has little or no direct control of subcontractors, he cannot control this major contributor to spiraling costs. On a typical construction project, 80 percent or more of the work is subcontracted to specialty trade contractors. Frequently, the owner is surprised when such subcontractors submit claims, through the GC, that the owner deems excessive, and usually his first response to such a claim is to withhold payment. But this drastic action is often neither contractually permitted nor in the project's best interests. Stopping payment to one subcontractor can result in immediate delays that will further adversely impact the overall cost. The first sub stops work, and its stoppage prevents others from working but the others continue to pile up hours that need to be paid for. And so on and on.

Another problem for owners comes when GC's submit claims for "extras." It is not uncommon for information about alternative construction procedures or materials to become known after the bid phase. But by this point in the building cycle, changes that earlier would have been simple to accommodate now represent opportunities for new claims by contractors and subs—claims that go by the name of "extras." Unfortunately, in such situations, the owner is usually faced with the GC and subcontractors who, to protect or enhance their profits, offer less in terms of "credits" and charge him excessively more for these changes. Without sufficient expertise on board, the owner is unlikely to find a factual basis for rejecting such claims.

## Developing the CM Approach

In the 1950s and 1960s, I was able to see and understand the problems that arose between owners and GCs perhaps more acutely than other developers or contractors were able to, because as an owner/builder doing construction for our family's portfolio, I was able to avoid many common pitfalls. For example, Tishman Realty & Construction did not as often run into the problem of shifting designs in the midst of the construction phase or, on the construction side, of employing a GC that needed to cut corners in order to make a profit.

Because of the way in which Tishman Realty grew in the 1960s, I had the opportunity to build more buildings than most general contractors, and to do so for the benefit of the owners. The process that I labeled Construction Management is essentially what we at Tishman Construction had been doing for Tishman Realty—managing the construction.

As I have described in an earlier chapter, the first opportunity for managing came in supervising the linked construction of the Garden and Two Penn Plaza. For that project, we were paid a fee that was a small percentage of the total construction budget. Coming at this task from the point of view of owner-builders, we looked for ways to slim down the construction time, and to use the best systems—those that would lower later operating costs—because every nickel saved and week of construction that we did not have to do was reflected in our bottom line and in the bottom lines of our partners.

In a sense, we in Tishman Construction were performing the supervisory tasks that a general contractor would do, but we were doing these tasks from a position *on the same side of the table as the owners,* working with them instead of, as a GC must do, negotiating against them. This meant, for example, that we did not have to find ways to make a little extra money from the owner on Part A of the project as a result of having underestimated a cost in Part B and would lose money on that—because we were not struggling to make a profit as a contracting entity; rather, we were managers, being paid a fee for our expertise and our supervisory services.

We became a construction entity that built for an owner as though we were part of the owner's team. In the Madison Square Garden project, the Felts had, in effect, rented the Tishman Construction division, and my construction division colleagues and I functioned as the Felts' employees although we did so from our own Tishman offices.

That was why, right after the MSG project, I was able to successfully argue to my uncles that our construction division should be allowed to look for other such fee-based opportunities to manage construction projects for others. They agreed, and let me take our owner/builder approach to Construction Management to school, so to speak, with projects for the University of Ohio, New York University, and the University of Illinois.

The third one was particularly significant for the history of CM, because it required us to convince the federal government, whose funds were being used to finance the university library, that CM was not only permissible in federal contracts but desirable.

## Selling the Federal Government on the CM Idea

The University of Illinois project involved the SOM firm—and did so mainly because SOM had gotten into trouble by agreeing not only to design the building but to supervise the construction for a fixed price, which I recall was around $12 million. They had set this price before bids because the federal government was involved, and the agency in charge had insisted that designs be completed, and that SOM (or some other firm) would have to guarantee the price before the money could be made available to the university. However, after SOM signed this contract, when they solicited bids for the construction based on their approved drawings, the estimates came in at around $17 million. At this point, they called me and we looked over the designs with an eye toward bringing down the price of construction. After our internal review, I told SOM that if they could convince the university and the government to allow certain design changes, the building could

*The Regenstein Library at the University of Chicago, our first Construction Management project involving federal government funds.*

be constructed for less than $12 million. These design changes were basic, structural ones, and really should have been the basis for the original plans. The various parties agreed to the alteration, the building was constructed, and it met everyone's expectations.

Before that project, the General Services Administration, through its building division, had insisted on all projects being done in that old way. Specs for designs were drawn up, and these went sent out for bids. An architectural firm was selected, and then designs were made and approved in-house, usually after a couple of rounds of back and forth with the bureaucrats. Only after designs were completed were they sent out to general contractors for bids. Then a construction contract would be awarded and construction would begin. Among the problems with this cumbersome, step-by-small-step approach is that it lengthened the time required to do a project by anywhere from six months to two years.

We argued to PBS, the Public Building Service, that it was possible to begin the foundations before a building was completely designed, because the foundations could be constructed knowing what the approximate weight of that superstructure would be—and that this would save money by reducing the total time of construction, and that it would not adversely impact the design process. This was the approach that, after some wrangling, and visits to Washington, the PBS had agreed to let us try on the University of Illinois library. After that building was completed—on budget and on a tight schedule—all the parties involved could see that we had saved time and money, and, in consequence, the government began to switch over to CM for many of its future projects.

Our firm completed projects as Construction Manager both for private owners and for public entities. The main difference between private and public projects, for us, is that on private projects we are always acutely conscious of the identity of the owner, and we work as part of that owner's team. In public-sector projects, the "client" is usually an institution, not an individual, and often there is no single individual to whom we can refer for the many decisions that need to be made during construction, sometimes on a daily basis. Often, on a public-sector job, because of the absence of such a single decision-maker, we end up taking an even larger role than we do in a private-sector project.

What the PBS especially liked in the CM approach was the scheduling—it put a lot of information on paper, where people could look at it and understand how a project could progress, and, while construction was ongoing, how much progress was being made from week to week, if not from day to day.

The scheduling aspects of the CM discipline became central to how we functioned as Construction Managers on several public sector projects as well as the Hancock Center, Renaissance Center, and the twin World Trade Center towers. By the end of the 1960s, I had convinced many decision makers that in the future, all major construction ought to be supervised by means of the Construction Management approach.

*The Jacob Javits Federal Building in Foley Square, Manhattan,
one of our many public-sector projects after we convinced the Public
Buildings Service of the CM approach.*

## *Being Professional about It*

Perhaps the most important difference between CM and general contracting is that the Construction Manager is a professional who possesses an expertise and who relates to the client in a manner exactly like that of other professionals—doctors, lawyers, architects, and accountants. When as a client you go to a doctor, you don't shop around for the lowest bidder of medical services, you seek out the best and you don't argue with the doctor about his or her fee. Ditto, when you engage a lawyer. Whether the lawyer charges you as the client $100 per hour or $200 per hour is less important to you than whether the lawyer is expert enough in his or her field. When a client chooses someone to manage his or her construction project, the process should be similar: the client should look for someone who knows what he or she is doing, not for the lowest bidder who can provide the service.

Our professionalism was the clinching argument, I believe, on a key private project for us, Texaco's northeast headquarters. It came about in the early 1970s, when we were looking for an anchor tenant for the Tishman public corporation's 1166 Sixth Avenue. We learned that Texaco was planning to move out of its corporate headquarters in the Chrysler Building and was looking for substantial office space in New York. But when I discovered that the president and chairman of Texaco seemed inclined toward moving the headquarters to the northern suburbs where they each lived, rather than staying in Manhattan, I shifted my goal to becoming the Construction Manager for their new building. But first I had to make my case.

Someone suggested to me that the best moment to approach the executives was during their annual convention in Houston, and I flew down to Texas for that purpose. One of their top vice-presidents asked me to wait in my room for a call to a meeting that would happen around nine in the evening, after their annual banquet. By eleven that evening, when no one had called me, I decided that the meeting was not going to take place and put on my pajamas. Not five minutes later the call came, and in my haste to get to the meeting I put my clothes on over my pajamas. Those awaiting me included the president, the CEO, and a slightly lower-ranked executive named Jim Dunlap, who clearly knew more than the others about construction.

I made my spiel, and could tell from the body language and the questions of the executives that they responded best to my assertion that we would be providing to them a professional service in the same way that we provided it for projects that we were building for the portfolio of Tishman Realty & Construction.

They agreed to hire us. I was particularly appreciative of the opportunity to build for Texaco, as it broke a barrier—a religious-based one. Prior to this time, most major industrial and financial corporations had been reluctant to award professional work to firms with Jewish owners.

But my major selling point to Texaco was that in our role as Construction Manager, we would act for them as a professional lawyer or accountant does, as their agent. We would sit with them on the same side of the table and would negotiate on their behalf with contractors and subcontractors. This posture was memorialized in the language of our CM contracts, which calls for the owner to rent our firm, to take it temporarily into his or her own, so that for the duration of the project we become, in effect, temporary employees of the owner.

In some ways, this posture meant Construction Managers taking over as the owner's agent from architects, who were used to being the only building-industry professionals on the owner's side of the table. In the 1960s, when we began this approach to supervising construction, architects were uncomfortable with us having this role, as they believed we were displacing them. We weren't—not entirely. We were simply joining the team on the owner's side of the table. But that meant the architects were not the only building-industry professionals advising the owner, and it sometimes meant that we would critique the architect's plans in a way that the architect did not like. In some ways, I thought the architects' uneasiness about our presence was a residue of class consciousness. Architects had always considered themselves as belonging to the upper class—the owner class—while they simulta-

*The idea of Construction Management sealed the deal for us to*
*supervise the construction of Texaco's new headquarters.*

neously viewed those who did the actual construction work, the general contractors and subs, the trades, as members of the lower class. I believe that distinction to be wrong, and that it should never be made. Furthermore, history shows that it is not warranted. In the master builder era, the architect and construction supervisor were either the same person or they were working collaboratively on the project, as were the trades, so in that sense all of them were from the same class.

Tishman Construction was ideally suited to utilize the Construction Management approach because we knew from an owner's perspective over the course of seventy years where the action in a construction project would be, and we were therefore better able to alert an owner client to those places and moments than, say, a reconstructed GC firm or a CM division of an architecture firm might have been. What owner-builders do is take risks, and others owners appreciated our sensitivity to the risks they were taking on their construction projects, and what we would do to minimize their exposure to construction problems and cost escalations.

## *Who Likes CM and Who Doesn't Like CM*

Owners like Construction Management, and by owners I also mean top executives of firms whose main business is not real estate, such as the CEOs of firms that want to build headquarters and such. I saw this, first-hand, in working with Henry Ford, Jr. on Renaissance Center. Mr. Ford was always respectful of the professionals engaged in this massive building project, architect John Portman and myself. CM appeals to CEOs because we work as managers, in a way similar to what they do, and we do it as their temporary, "in-house" employees.

The list of who might not like Construction Management, in my view, validates why CEOs and private business owners should like it.

Principal among those annoyed by the CM approach are architects, because Construction Managers have the standing to say "no" to the architects' extravagances or, more frequently, to suggest substituting a more practical design instead of one that will primarily enhance the architect's own brochure and will not necessarily be advantageous for the client. The inherent conflict between architects and CMs came to the fore as the CM approach was developed. Shortly, in response, large architectural firms began their own construction management departments in an attempt to recapture some of this territory for themselves; but after a few years, those in-house CM departments began to fade away because they had been fatally compromised from the get-go. The job of a CM is to rein in excessive costs and to question the appropriateness of various design ideas, in order to help the client control costs during the construction phase and also the costs of future maintenance. But architects want to be unhampered, and at day's end architectural firms' CM departments were just too compromised by the designers of the architectural firm, and so could not provide the best advice to their clients.

The second group of people who dislike CM are middle-rank construction executives at large corporations, especially those corporations that are not in the real estate business. The chief of construction at such a firm often feels that his fiefdom is challenged by a Construction Manager who talks directly with his boss, the CEO. Also, at times these construction chiefs have overly cozy relationships with con-tractors. In some instances, I have had to tell CEOs that their construc-tion chiefs were on the take or, more often, that the construction chiefs were throwing up roadblocks to our progress; more than once, such a conversation (and the information that backed it up) resulted in some-one being fired. However, most of the time we were able to develop a working relationship with an in-house construction chief that enabled him or her to see us properly as an ally rather than as a rival.

The third group that doesn't like CM is the subcontractors. Here, too, the problem has been the bid-rigging and sweetheart deals on which some subcontractors relied during the old GC days. It was relatively easy for, say, the few large sheetmetal subcontractors to get together and decide which of them would be low bidder on the next available job. But that bid-rigging relationship was short-circuited by the existence of Construction Managers, who while working for the client are not obligated to accept the lowest bidder for a particular job; as a CM we could, and frequently did, select subcontractors—with the owner's representative sitting by our side—on the basis of which one presented the best overall package. Often, we would ask subcontractors for their best ideas on how to provide alternative materials or ways of fulfilling a particular design requirement or to effect cost savings, and on the basis of their answers we would recommend hiring the one with the most innovative package of experience, tools, and ideas.

## *The Team Approach and Fast Tracking*

From the start of the design process, through construction and occu-pancy, the Construction Manager has work to do, arranging for the selection of, and coordinating the contributions of, required special-ists, engineers, trades-people, and suppliers. Often we as a CM are even involved in the selection of an architect and in the supervision of the design work.

As the letter from the CMAA, quoted above, points out, the CM approach that we pioneered, which involved the combined and coordinated efforts of owner, architect, and construction expert, is a true *team* approach. Through this approach, and well ahead of the actual construction, both the owner and the architect can have all the necessary resources to analyze design and system alternatives and their impact on costs and schedules. Our work makes the owner most completely aware of aesthetic, schedule, and cost trade-offs *before* making design and program decisions.

Along with practical design critiques, scheduling is the CM's greatest contribution to the building process. Scheduling is equivalent to building the job on paper. In the early days of computers, we developed our T-COM system for construction scheduling together with the aircraft manufacturer McDonnell Douglas. We were constantly sending material back and forth with their big mainframe computer in St. Louis in an attempt to compose and edit our schedules. Later, we bought our own mainframe, which quickened the pace of schedule-making. Scheduling is not the beginning of the construction process, nor does it take place in a vacuum; rather, the schedules are the concrete expression of the pre-production dialogues among the key personnel on a project, including the architect, various engineers, the owner, and the CM as manager of the entire process.

Once the overall design and production schedules are agreed upon, and with the Construction Manager acting as the general supervisor, each segment of the construction is contracted for between the CM, serving as the owner's agent, and the individual trade contractors. With such an approach, no single trade contractor will have the ability to unduly hold up the job and therefore squeeze more money out of the owner. If need be, using a CM approach any individual contractor or subcontractor can be replaced without radically or negatively affecting the whole job. Even though the CM firm acts as the hiring entity, it should attempt to take a collaborative approach in working with subcontractors so that all can try their best to get the job done. The idea is not for the CM to crack the whip like overseers to get the subs to work productively; rather, CMs should act as orchestra conductors who mesh the products of all the individual violinists, bassoonists, and drummers to make the production happen, and happen smoothly.

An integral part of the CM approach is "fast tracking." This means that design and construction phases can proceed simultaneously, overlapping, as we had done with the University of Illinois library, sinking the foundations before the redesign of the superstructure was complete. Such procedures produce major savings in time, and in construction, time saved equals money saved. More time is saved when the CM gives out appropriate parts of a project whenever possible, rather than bidding everything at once. Savings comes, too, from good coordination of materials delivery and of workmen at the job site, which is part of what a good CM does for a client.

Tishman Research did a study, for the Public Buildings Service of the General Services Administration, comparing the time schedules and other factors in 100 building projects in and around major cities, as done by CM and GC approaches to construction. They found that when a CM was involved in a project from design phase to completion, the amount of time saved by the CM approach was 30 percent. The earlier in the design phase that the CM was involved, the greater the savings of time and money.

The biggest bang for the bucks for the owner comes through engaging a CM firm very early in the process, sometimes even before the architect is picked, or at least well before that architect has completed preliminary designs.

Sometimes an architect, given free rein, will create a design that looks good on a small-scale model but that will be difficult or extra costly to construct. Conversely, some architects are more attuned to the needs of construction, and of the owner's need not to overspend, than others. When we are asked to recommend an architectural firm for a project—a frequent request—we are likely to suggest a firm known to us for its willingness to control costs and its willingness to adapt its designs to practical construction considerations, rather than an architect who refuses to be bothered by such considerations.

Most good CM firms, like ours, have on staff their own architectural, mechanical, and structural specialists. Having worked on all types of buildings in all sorts of situations, the good CM firm has usually amassed a corporate body of expertise, and top-notch specialists in each area, far beyond that of any individual owner's in-house team. Moreover, because of that broad expertise, a Construction Manager is also in a position to advise on such matters as site selection, and to assist in matters of zoning and environmental impact.

Overall, by using a CM approach, owners are usually able to save between six and eighteen months of construction time. This has benefits beyond the dollar savings. Shortening the time frame for construction allows the owner to lessen the potentially negative impact of market shifts that may occur between the time of conception and the time of completion. Such shortening also increases the owner's ability to shift objectives in mid-stream, should market conditions change radically—for instance, to alter what began as an office project to instead feature residences, or vice-versa.

## The Three-Legged Stool

"Who's in charge here, Tishman or me?" I can't tell you how many meetings with clients I've been in where that question was asked. Mid-level construction chiefs in non-real estate companies would ask it, big-time contractors would ask it, and, most of all, architects during the early days of CM would ask it. Posing the question was an indication that the questioner was likely to be on an ego trip, wanted to be the boss, and did not want the CM firm unduly influencing the client to modify anything that the asker was doing or proposing.

Usually, once we get over the tug-of-war between architect and CM, projects go pretty well. We have to, because on every job, construction is done by means of a three-legged stool—or so I never tire of telling the participants in client meetings. One leg consists of the owner and his staff, another leg features the architect and the design team, and the third leg is made up of the construction trades. The stool cannot stand on one or even on two legs, and cannot function properly unless all the legs are jointly supporting the job and one another. Certainly, the CM firm is part of the owner's team, and that is its major function, but the CM firm should also become a part of the design team by contributing its expertise on what is possible, feasible, and cost effective, and it should also be part of the construction team through its supervisory and coordination efforts. In truth, a CM should function as the glue that holds the stool together.

## Carnegie Hall Renovation

A prime example of CM in action was the project of renovating and restoring New York's famous Carnegie Hall, the country's best-known venue for classical music. As the hall approached its hundredth anniversary, the director and the board saw a need to completely renovate the concert facility. My associate Mike Mennella and I were summoned to the hall's office, and the directors handed us a heavy large-format book containing many, many drawings; it was a plan for what they wanted Carnegie Hall's various facilities and exterior to look like in seven years' time. But construction could only be done, during those seven years, in twenty-six-week spurts—or else, violinist Isaac Stern warned us, the Vienna Philharmonic and other groups wouldn't come back to its New York venue for their next season.

Our way of dealing with this restriction was to carve up the job into tasks that could be done in one of those short-burst periods. Year one, we'd tackle the basement and foundations; year two, the recital and rehearsal halls; year three, the exterior; year four, the main concert hall—and so on. By the time we were finished planning, we'd dissected

*Zankel Hall, one of our many projects in the restoration of Carnegie Hall. It had been a theater until the 1960s, and a cinema until 1997.*

their big seven-year vision book into bite-size, accomplishable portions of work. During each twenty-six-week burst, construction would go on around the clock, with materials being delivered at all hours.

The Carnegie Hall renovation project was considered an important innovation in the process of building; for me, it was also a spiritually meaningful project because of all the wonderful music I had heard over the decades at Carnegie.

Prior to this project, our firm had not done much in the way of renovations; we were used to building entirely new structures. Working within a hundred-year-old building venerated by many people was not easy for our crews, but we managed.

The old Carnegie Hall's glory was the sound that it produced; musicians loved it and so did the audiences. But when the newly renovated hall opened, some musicians were very upset because the stage seemed to be too hard, and some orchestra members did not feel the usual vibrations made by their colleagues during the course of playing.

Seeking a culprit, they blamed the flooring—specifically, what they believed to be concrete under the floor. And that, they believed, was the fault of Tishman Construction.

The rumor—for it was only a rumor, not reality—spread like wildfire and was very difficult to refute. There was something extra hard about the floors, and it had affected the sound. *The New York Times* printed an article that said just that, so it must be true!

People also claimed they had seen concrete trucks at Carnegie in the middle of the night, and that we had poured the stuff on the sly. Others claimed that they had actually seen concrete under the floors.

Neither claim was true. What looked like concrete under the stage was the original grout, which held upright the 100-year old wooden two-by-fours on which the floor rested. As for the trucks, what people had seen were trucks delivering other materials, not concrete.

*The New York Times* and other news outlets' reports of concrete deliveries notwithstanding, the idea of concrete was patently ridiculous, for several reasons. First, there had been no requirement in the stage floor design for concrete. Second, to have put in the amount of concrete that would have been needed to underlay the whole floor would have required concrete trucks delivering the stuff night and day, eighteen loads of it. Also, because of the structure of the building, to deliver eighteen truckloads of concrete would have meant countless wheelbarrows shutting back and forth to the street. Third, there were never any bills sent or paid for such concrete. We put out publicity to this effect, but it did not serve to dispel the rumors. Moreover, the hall's director, who knew the truth, did not dismiss the concrete rumors as vehemently as he might have done, leaving a lingering doubt in many people's minds. This doubt was heightened later on when Carnegie Hall put out a press release saying that the concrete had been removed!

There was none to be removed, but the actual explanation for the problem was embarrassing for Carnegie Hall, and therefore was not addressed. The architect's design had called for the underfloor to be laminated. That had been done, but as a result, the underfloor had become more like rock than like wood. It was the extra hardness of the laminating that produced the acoustical problem. When in later years the underfloor was removed and a new, unlaminated one substituted, the sound quality of the hall improved.

Even so, for years afterward I heard about the concrete; the rumor cost us at least one assignment that I know of, and perhaps others, too.

The Carnegie Hall Board of Trustees was happy with Tishman Construction's performance on the renovation. I know that because after we completed the "miracle," on time and on budget, I was asked to join that board and remained on it for the next two decades. Also, Tishman Construction was awarded contracts to do several other important renovations for Carnegie, for the Rainbow Room atop Rockefeller Center, an equally difficult and prodigious task, and for the South Street Seaport.

## *The Upside-Down Solution*

Concrete was also at the heart of the matter in another interesting CM project in Manhattan, what became Olympic Tower, across from St. Patrick's Cathedral and Rockefeller Center at 51st Street and Fifth Avenue. The site had been occupied for many years by a Best's department store, and had recently been bought by an old friend and client, Arthur Cohen of Arlen Real Estate. Cohen had had us build a Kmart mall in Yonkers when he had been CEO of Kmart, and now he wanted us to construct his new building. Arlen Real Estate also owned a concrete company, and that became part of the story.

His partner on the site, who owned a property adjacent to Best's in which he had had his New York headquarters, was Aristotle Onassis, the Greek shipping and airlines magnate. Olympic was the name of his airline, and that would give the building its name.

The two men had formed an equal partnership and hired SOM to design a building. Before that process was complete, Cohen wanted to hire us as Construction Managers.

There was a wrinkle, though. A real estate construction consultant to the Port Authority and to Pan Am wanted to recommend us to Onassis. So I was in the enviable position of being recommended to both partners in a venture. But the consultant wanted me to represent only the Onassis interests, not the Arlen interests.

The first big question to be answered, in terms of construction processes, was whether the building should be steel or concrete. Steel is usually recommended for office buildings, and concrete for residential buildings; concrete floor construction actually has better sound dampening qualities than steel, and can better absorb sound so that the noises from one apartment and floor will not bother tenants in the next apartment. Since this was to be a mixed-use building, offices on the lower floors and luxury apartments above, we might have used either system. Onassis, heavily involved in the shipping business, favored steel; Arlen owned a concrete subcontractor.

In sum: Arlen wanted an all-concrete building, while SOM (and Onassis) wanted an all-steel building.

After listening to all the input about the building's structural design and uses, I recommended to both partners that we use an upside-down, reverse structure, with concrete for the offices part of the building and steel for the residential part. Since the apartments were to be rather large and well separated from each other, the need for concrete's dampening qualities was diminished. Steel, lighter and more flexible, would aid in apartment design. Below, concrete's structural qualities would enhance the utility of the office floors and lobby display area. Underneath that lobby, there was to be a museum for Hellenic art, and the walls of the lobby, a public space, would need to be open and strong enough to display replicas of the Elgin Marbles, as well as containing a waterfall and space for cafés. To properly support the open spaces and the structures above, large columns would be required.

Both partners pronounced themselves satisfied with this upside-down solution. I breathed a sigh of relief and thereafter, we represented both owners, without problems.

Design sessions on the building were a treat for me, as Mrs. Onassis, the former Jacqueline Kennedy, attended a number of design sessions, as did Mr. Onassis. While she contributed her ideas to the interior designs of the luxury apartments, he seemed most interested in the overall design process.

# SEVEN

# *Being a Leader*

Having been the leader of a company for a long time, and having dealt with a substantial number of leaders of other large private companies, I have evolved a few principles and observations about leadership that I believe can be useful to everyone in daily life.

## *Let's* Not *Split the Difference*

Often enough, in a meeting, we will come to an impasse, say over the efficacy of a design. I'll want it this way and another person at the table will want it a different way—and someone (other than me) will say, "Let's split the difference."

Let's not. No way. If I'm correct in my position, why should I compromise? My task is to convince the other person, by logic, of the correctness of my position. Does my stance on not splitting the difference mean that I'm stubborn? Certainly I am when I know I'm right. And I know when that is, because I generally can back up my position with reasons and evidence drawn from experience.

If I say the design of the door needs to be forty inches wide to accommodate a wheelchair, and the person opposite me at the table says that a thirty-six-inch wide door frame is more aesthetically pleasing, what purpose would it serve to "split the difference" between the two dimension recommendations? None, in my view.

By the way, my experience in this world has taught me that people don't get far in business unless they believe they are right and will stick to their guns. Being a "yes"-man to a boss will take you only part way toward the top.

Of course, there are times when I've been right but I don't win the argument. In such cases, I am content because I have pointed out to the client what would be the benefits of doing something in the way that I recommended versus the way chosen by someone else, usually the architect. A good example is the Los Angeles Century City triangular building known as the "theme complex." Architect Minoru Yamasaki wanted no columns between the triangular vertices on the first floor, an expanse of more than 200 feet, to create the effect that the more than 40 stories of office floors appear to be held up by just three end-point columns. I argued two counts with the architect and with Alcoa, the owners of Century City. One, we could achieve the same effect from the exterior view by having several columns in the middle of each side of the triangle; they would not be visible from the exterior because they would surely be hidden by drapes. Two, that having only three columns at the apexes would be very costly, since we would have to first construct a "Vierendeel" truss system across each of the three façades, extending from the second floor to the top of the building. This would delay the construction of the individual floors until we had finished the truss. If there were columns in the middle, there would be no need for a truss system, and we could pour those concrete floors as we built toward the sky.

I lost the argument. Alcoa chose to do it Yamasaki's way and we proceeded with the construction, putting in the Vierendeel truss system so that there are only columns at the apexes. Doing things that way cost a whole lot more than if we had put in interior columns, but Alcoa was willing to foot the expense.

The kicker for me, though, is that the vast expanses at the first floor, under the trusses and between the three legs of the triangular building, cannot be appreciated from the outside anyway, because—as I suspected would happen—window drapes and office partitions were installed along the entire length of the building.

Nonetheless, I was content because I had made the argument and my points had been understood. The architect and owner simply chose to go another way, but they did so knowing the true cost of the open floors would be extraordinary and, more importantly, the project would require many extra months to build, since no interior work could commence until the truss system had been completed at roof level.

## Intuition—Trusting Yourself

I feel vs. I think.

In the old days, Uncle Norman and I would regularly have conversations in which I'd say, "I feel that we ought to do it this way," and he would invariably answer, "What do you mean—'you feel'? Say 'I think.' Either you have logical reasons for making a recommendation, or you don't."

Norman considered himself to be a very logical man; he did so because when he had to make a decision, he'd write out on a yellow pad all of the reasons pro and con, some of them gathered from "outside opinions," and when in his mind one side of the page outweighed the other, he'd go with that option.

To me, his process was overly analytical. Just because the "con" side of the ledger might be more full than the "pro" side, in terms of lines on the page, did not mean that you have correctly evaluated and weighted every factor. Some factors may be much more important than others. Overanalysis does not, I believe, lead to the best decisions.

I'm a logical person, too, and I regularly apply logic to situations that call for decisions, but I never write out my reasons for making the decision. I can't, because not all of my "reasons" are logic-based. Many of the elements on which I rely are sensations or nonverbal clues; these latter are very important, for instance, in reaching a decision about choosing a candidate for a job.

Actually, my objection to solely relying on logic goes deeper than that. When I say, "I feel," I mean precisely that I have a feeling in my gut, not a physical ache but nevertheless a sensation strong enough to send me a message, an instinctual, persuasive message telling me that one or the other direction is the right one to go in.

Some people call it playing their hunches. I call it intuition.

In business, intuition has a bad rap. But my belief about decisions, born of experience, is that all decisions are essentially intuitive, and that each intuitive decision is made up of smaller "mini-intuitions" that cumulatively give rise to that sensation that I feel in my gut about the best way to go. Most of these mini-intuitions are not quite conscious ones, and they come from clues in the environment that we are not always aware of understanding or of reacting to. But the clues exist, and we must pay attention to them rather than ignore our intuition-based decisions. We can always look for "proof," but my sense of the proof provided by outside experts is that, more often than not, it, too, is just another opinion.

Recently, scientists have begun to find that trusting your gut instincts is a good idea. "We may actually know more than we think we know in everyday situations," said a Northwestern University neuroscientist after doing a research study. "Intuition may have an important role in finding answers to all sorts of problems."

In matters such as evaluating whom to trust, intuition is everything. Résumés and recommendation letters don't tell you everything that you need to know to make a decision about that person, and certainly not all that you may obtain from direct contact and interaction with him or her. An in-person session provides lots of clues about someone's trustworthiness, confidence, and competence.

"A fact is a fact," people are fond of saying; they use that notion as rationale for decision-making that is deliberately non-intuitive. Yes, some facts are provable—a stone is a stone—but many things in life that are passed off as facts are actually impressions of what is true or real, and they are subject to interpretation. I believe, accordingly, that all decisions, even those supposedly based only on facts, are at bottom intuitive.

Trusting my intuition has helped to make my career a successful one; I have often made choices based on my gut feelings, and have been rewarded in consequence.

The important concept here is trusting your intuition. Let's suppose, for the sake of argument, that choices based on logic are correct only 50 percent of the time. If intuition, added to logic, gains you an extra 1 percent, then you will be right more times than others who don't add a factor for intuition. That added 1 percent difference can certainly be the margin necessary for success, particularly since you have to make many, many decisions, about matters large and small, every minute of every waking hour of your life.

Does this mean trusting first impressions? Not necessarily. Some people believe in the correctness of their first impressions, while others use a longer time period for evaluation. What makes the positive difference is trusting the impression, no matter how long it may take you to reach it. When that impression crystallizes, seize it and act accordingly.

It is hard for me to precisely express this, but I believe strongly that trusting one's own intuition is a foundation for success in any endeavor.

I'm also a believer in what I call "negative intuition," by which I mean the act of deliberately not trusting one's own intuition. I've seen negative intuition in action many times in other people, and have become convinced that negative intuition is what prevents people from achieving at the highest levels. Their intuition may tell them what to do, but they don't trust their gut and so, very often, they make the *opposite* choice, deciding to go 180 degrees away from what their gut tells them. Quite often, this counterintuitive choice brings them no joy.

I'm certain that you, too, have encountered such reflexively counterintuitive people: after dealing with them once or twice, you can count on whatever they say or do to be mostly the wrong thing, the very opposite of what should be said or done. To me, such bad decisions are the mark of someone who has succumbed to "negative intuition." This negative attitude only worsens as the individual ages and continues to resist following his first impressions because he or she feels those impressions have so often been wrong in the past.

Using your intuition in a positive way is also connected integrally to risk-taking; I even go so far as to assert that people take risks in proportion to their willingness to trust their intuitive sense of things. To become better at risk-taking—which is integral to many business decisions—I have always advised friends and relatives to trust their intuition. It is central to good decision-making and to successful risk-taking.

In the fields of real estate and construction, perhaps more so than in many other arenas of business, every project is a calculated risk. Nothing is 100 percent "safe." So leadership in those fields becomes a matter of managing risk, controlling the gambles insofar as possible. Risk is absolutely necessary to achieving rewards. The greater the risks, generally, the greater the potential rewards.

## *A Win Based on Intuition*

We had become experienced in developing hotels for our own portfolio, having done so successfully with two hotels in Chicago and one in Puerto Rico, in addition to the three at Disney World. That experience spurred us to have our firm enter a competition to develop a site at Eighth Avenue and 42nd Street on which New York City's Times Square Redevelopment Authority decided there ought to be a new hotel. In Construction Management, we competed for jobs but had never done so by competitive bidding; a client either wanted us as Construction Managers, or they wanted to use some other process. In terms of hotels, we had previously sought opportunities that did not involve competitive bids. But this proposed project, on what had been a decrepit corner of 42nd Street, near the Port Authority's bus terminal, was a great opportunity, and I thought we could win the bidding. The hotel entrance would be on 43rd Street, but the building would take up the entire east side of the block of Eighth Avenue between 42nd and 43rd.

The 42nd Street corridor had been an entertainment haven since the latter part of the 19th century and would remain so. The Redevelopment Authority was working hard to upgrade it, to get rid of the pornographic film theaters and sex-related retail shops. The winning bid would have to include how we would develop the low-lying space along 42nd as well as the configuration for a major hotel on the site. We came up with a concept we called E-Walk, for several hundred thousand square feet of street-level stores along 42nd Street, and an 810-room hotel to be entered from both 42nd Street and 43rd Street.

My intuition told me that the way to win the hotel bid was to embrace the entertainment aspects of 42nd Street. From that initial decision, several others flowed. The first was to go into this bid with Disney as a partner. In this period Disney was thinking about building its own chain of Vacation Clubs. This was during the period when we were involved with Disney in rebuilding the New Amsterdam Theater. We worked through a concept that would allot Disney 200 of the proposed hotel's 800 rooms for their New York City Vacation Club, rooms that would also be available to the general public when not occupied by Disney clients. Later on, that, too, fell through, but the notion of having a Disney-style hotel stayed with us. It led to our second intuition-based decision. Because our main competitors for the site were the big hotel chains, I figured that the only way we could win was to have our design be more entertaining, and more 42nd Street-ish than most of them would be comfortable suggesting, and for that purpose, we engaged as our architects a firm that had done considerable work for Disney, Arquitectonica of Miami. I was particularly impressed that their past design work, while very creative, was also generally rectangular at the base, a necessity for New York City, where, to be viable, a structure must fill every square inch of land.

*E-Walk and its associated hotel have revitalized
the Times Square-42nd Street area.*

We told the architects that we wanted something jazzy and reflective of 42nd Street's history as the city's entertainment center. We were going to have to spend a lot of money to win this prize, pay for a multitude of designs and models, and also work to satisfy the regulators—the site was under the jurisdiction of New York State as well as New York City. We were going to have financial partners, as well as involving the Westin Hotel chain as eventual operators—they, too, wanted a say in the design. When the early Arquitectonica sketches came in, my partners objected to them as too over-the-top, too glitzy, not enough like a "real" hotel. I loved the designs, and eventually prevailed on my partners to accept them as the best way to win the competition.

Long story somewhat shortened: after plowing through endless applications and making supporting documents—an entire five-foot shelf of them—we won the competition. The resulting hotel and entertainment center are not only spectacular but profitable for us,

*The Westin Hotel.*

for our partners, and for the city and state of New York, who share in the revenue from it.

## *Leadership and Choices*

I think that the hotel story also demonstrates that the most important task of a leader is to pick a direction for a project, a company, or an occasion, and then to be an enthusiast for that direction. People need leaders, and leaders need to demonstrate their leadership by making positive choices and then backing them up.

It is more important for a leader to make a choice than to delay making one for any reason whatsoever, good or bad. This is especially true if you as the leader are uncertain as to the ultimate effect of the decision. Making that initial decision, no matter what it is, is vitally important because so many other items wait upon the making of the first decision.

For example, the decision that a particular property ought to be designed as an office building, not as an apartment complex or a hotel, has many ramifications. Making the top-level decision, quickly and positively, enables the completing of many decisions about details—how many floors there should be in the new building, how many square feet, how soon the supplies should be brought on-site, and so on. To put off making the top-level decision would be to keep all those other decisions in limbo, delaying everything. That's why I almost never say, when confronted with the need to make a decision, "I'll sleep on it."

To say you'll sleep on it is to communicate that you're vacillating, that you're unsure. Perhaps refusing to sleep on it is a fault of mine, but I prefer making the decision to seeming indecisive because I feel that the essence of being a leader is decisiveness. Also, when you "sleep on it" you are in effect denying your intuitive sense that will lead you to the right decision. Let me say this with emphasis: the answer you come up with in the morning, after sleeping on it, is very likely to be more conservative and less vigorous than what your gut told you was correct at the moment you needed to make that decision.

And—let me say boldly—it is more important to make a decision, any decision, even though you may have a sneaking suspicion that something may later prove your decision to have been wrong, than not to make a decision.

## *Reversing Yourself*

When circumstances change or when new facts emerge, a leader must be entirely willing to change direction, on a dime if necessary, to go 180 degrees from what he said or decided yesterday, and then to be equally enthusiastic about the new direction. Leaders must not be doctrinaire, which I define as hewing to a particular line of thought even after it has been shown to be inadequate to the task. "Do I contradict myself? Very well then, I contradict myself," Walt Whitman wrote. And, as Emerson once famously said, "A foolish consistency is the hobgoblin of little minds."

Consistency is important; "foolish consistency"—by which I take Emerson to mean unreasonable and doctrinaire consistency, isn't worth much.

The willingness to change one's mind when new information is added to the equation is, I've found, part of what defines good leadership. It is quite reasonable and not at all dilatory to reverse yourself: the basis on which you made the decision yesterday has either been shown to have been incomplete, or the equation has now been altered by the advent of better information—and so you change your mind.

People whose leadership styles I admire, such as Bob Kerrey, a former senator and current president of The New School, now and then made a decision and chose a direction, and sometime later, decided to do the opposite and were just as enthusiastic about the new direction.

Actually, one of the reasons that people such as Bob and myself have very little difficulty in making decisions in the first place is because we understand ourselves to be ready, willing, and able to reverse those decisions, with no embarrassment, should the need to do so arise because additional facts have come to our attention.

## *"The Dentist"*

I never thought of myself as a dentist, but some colleagues in Tishman Realty and Construction have described me that way. I found out what they mean: that during in-house sessions I ask questions of them, and keep on asking questions, until I am certain that they have the answers—I "drill down" until I reach the level at which they may not have completely thought out their answers, and sometimes, thereby, I reveal to them, and to myself, the weakness of our logic or evidence. I am then able to send them back to do more homework or re-examine the suppositions on which they based their recommendations. I'm perfectly willing to take, as a colleague's reason, that his gut tells him this is the right direction, but I want to understand his reasons insofar as it is possible to explain them. One of my most-asked questions, my colleagues tell me, is "What are you trying to accomplish?"

Drilling down for a solution to a problem is obviously a necessary process, because in order to defend our choices, decisions, and recommendations in meetings with outsiders, we need to be absolutely certain that we have gotten to—pardon the pun—the root of the problem and have properly dealt with it before presenting a decision.

I believe that what we mean when we say we trust someone is that we have satisfied ourselves that this person will have done his or her drilling homework to the point where you know that it does not require second-guessing on your part.

## *I'll Come to* Your *Office*

It has been rare for anyone to be fired at our company, but I had to let go an employee with long service, once, because the man, who was fairly high up in the management of the company, kept insisting that "subordinates" come to his office for meetings. He seemed to feel that it was beneath his dignity to go to any of their offices when they needed to discuss anything.

This sort of hierarchical behavior is, I believe, not good for companies. Other people in our company had grown weary of being treated by him not as colleagues but as people he ordered around.

I think of my own style of leadership as informal. In practice, this means that if I have something to discuss with you, I'd just as soon leave my office and go to yours and hope to chew it over with you there.

My informal style traces back to my childhood at the Walden School, where we were taught to address teachers by their first names— a great way to break down artificial barriers between teacher and students. I've always encouraged everyone in the company to call me

*Team spirit at Tishman Construction as we were finishing restoration of the New Amsterdam theater on 42nd Street.*

John; I kind of shivered if they addressed me as Mr. Tishman. My style also includes not wearing a tie most of the time, although of course I do dress more formally when going to meet a client for the first time, or on other appropriate occasions.

The point of the informality is to encourage collegiality. In our company, as in most companies, there is a great need for teamwork if we are to successfully complete multimillion-dollar projects for our clients. Given that objective, there is little room for hierarchical behavior, for concentrating on such silly matters as whose office has more windows.

## Reward and Challenge

In this era, when executives move from company to company every few years as they go up the ladder, and when loyalty between employer and employee has become an outmoded concept, I am proud that so many of my colleagues have worked for Tishman Construction for long stretches of time. Dozens have been with the company for more than twenty years, and we have quite a few second- and third-generation colleagues whose parents and grandparents were Tishman employees. Also, we have a very good retention rate, not losing many employees to other firms, coupled with a good rate of return—when a valued employee does move to another company for a while, he or she will often ask to return to Tishman Construction, preferring our style of doing business. We pride ourselves on performing Construction Management as a profession, not as a trade. That means we are all professional colleagues, a distinction that makes for quite a different company atmosphere than the one a former employee of ours may encounter when working for a general contractor, no matter how large the firm.

We would not have so many long-term employees or returnees if we were not recognizing and rewarding our people, promoting them, and steadily increasing their levels of responsibility. We provide incentives for those who take on the responsibility for their own and others' performance. Often, in substantial-size companies, the biggest problem in retaining a good young executive is creating challenging opportunities for their roads to advancement. In the middle levels of management, good people can become blocked by their supervisors' insecurities or general inadequacies. A number of times I have had to "unlock" a bright young career by moving aside another's career.

This was frequently made possible because a major client was working with the young executive, and was willing to let that young executive innovate but had sensed that the young man's superior was preventing him from fulfilling the client's desires. That paradigm made it easier for me to clear the young executive's path by getting his immediate superior out of the way—putting that man in another position, or even firing him if I had to. Moving young executives up in this manner is easier to do in a service business such as ours, where as Construction Managers we have continuous contact with our clients on their projects, than it might be in a manufacturing company.

But under any circumstances, when I realize that a bright young executive's career is being stifled, that provides me with a good reason to reassign or otherwise move out of the way anyone who is doing the stifling. No high executive should be getting in the way of his subordinates' growth.

A young man came to us right out of business school, as a summer intern in our real estate department. He was terrific on numbers and analyses of information in regard to just about everything to which he was assigned. Whenever I needed information, I would call the top man in his department and he would arrive with the information and with this young man, who, he said, had assisted in the preparation. After a few such conferences, it became obvious to me who had prepared and analyzed the information—the young man—and so I began calling him directly, sometimes waiting until the lunch hour to do so in order not to appear to be circumventing his boss. It also became clear that his boss was holding down this talent, and I took steps to free him. Later, as he rose quickly in the company, I had to do so a second time, so that he could continue to take on responsibilities commensurate with his talent and experience.

Employees can grow in expertise and confidence only if they are given the opportunity to meet a series of ever-greater challenges. Construction and real estate provide many chances to incrementally step up the level of challenge on successive jobs. One year, you'll be in charge of a $1 million piece of the business; the next year, on another job, we will be able to make you responsible for a bigger task on a project that has a higher price tag. If you perform well—meet the expectations—we can then reward you with more salary and promotions, and opportunities to continue to increase the level of your tasks.

I'm big on assigning specific responsibilities to executives and on having them do the same to their subordinates. I want them to give individuals control over certain sectors of a job, to make them individually responsible for that part of the project. I believe that employees at whatever level will do their jobs better when they have specific objectives that they can and must accomplish. They need very much to have the possibility of "owning" a particular segment of the work, because taking ownership is always important to an individual's growth and competence. I have always looked for and found methods of sharing the rewards, whether that takes the form of giving the responsible individual a portion of the savings on a construction project or a "piece of the action" in a real estate venture.

## Expertise vs. Salesmanship

Having sold my company's services to clients for more than fifty years, I feel that I know a lot about salesmanship, and I respect what a salesman does. But when I'm looking for advice, I don't want someone selling me, I want an expert advising me based on his or her experience, training, and general savvy. Experts are more productive and, I've found, easier to work with than salesmen.

The important thing is to recognize the difference between a salesman and an expert, since salespeople generally try to come on as though they are experts. They may have some expertise, but their basic posture—and sometimes their only talent—is selling something to you.

As Construction Managers we aim to provide to our clients a professional service based on expertise. I have always contended, to my colleagues and to our clients, that once we have made our agreement with the client we are no longer selling anything, and whatever recommendations we make are made as though we were providing the service to ourselves and would be reaping the benefit of the results. I often liken our service as Construction Managers to that of recognized professionals such as a doctor, lawyer, or CPA. Our clients must want us on their job because we are very good and very professional at what we do, not because our fees are higher or lower than some other firm's. It has always been a matter of pride to me for our firm to be selected to provide a service not because of a negotiated fee but rather because of our recognized track record of experience, expertise, and successfully completed projects.

## Getting that Repeat Business

Proof of the worth of Tishman Construction's expertise is that we are frequently asked to do second, third, and fourth projects for a particular company or developer. This characterized our relationship with Disney and with such important developers as Larry Silverstein and Bill Zeckendorf. To my mind, among the most important aspects of being a leader in a service business is taking charge of obtaining repeat business for your company. This includes making certain that your company performs well in its first contract with a client, but also carefully managing the client relationship so that all issues are addressed and not permitted to fester and possibly spoil the prospects for a second contract. To my mind, this mandates a leadership posture that lets one's clients know that they can call the top guy handling their project, or the leader of the company, at any time. It also mandates that part of the leader's job is devoted to making sure that the client is fully satisfied with the quality of the service and that it meets the client's expectations. The leader of a service company should establish contact with the client's company as near to the top as allowed by the chief officer and his subordinates, and should maintain that contact throughout all the stages of the project, and even afterward. I have found that it is critical not to permit a middle manager of a client to shield the higher-ups from knowing what problems are occurring on the job site until it is too late to properly remediate the problems. Continual communication with the highest client level possible is the best way to avoid such difficulties.

## *Passing the Torch*

An important aspect of a CEO's responsibilities is succession planning, to assure the continuity and success of the company after he leaves or retires.

For many years, I had a successor in mind, but could do little about it. My only son, Dan, had had a varied career, part of it as a teacher (like his father), and including a master's degree as an environmentalist, before moving to Maine and to a small farm on which he and his wife Sheryl raised llamas. To renovate their antique farmhouse, Dan hired a small general contractor and helped supervise the job. Afterward, he joined forces with the GC and became a principal of a company that did environmentally conscious renovations of large estates.

At one of the Tishman Construction annual Christmas parties, two of my firm's senior partners—dispatched by me—talked to Dan about coming into the firm now that he had gotten his feet wet in the construction business. Dan said that he had no ambition to follow in my footsteps and that Sheryl, who was from Maine and loved New England, did not like New York City and would surely not agree to move there.

Nonetheless, discussions went back and forth for a while and eventually, in 1990, Dan consented to taking a job with Tishman Construction—but only in our New England office, and only during the week. He rented an apartment in Boston and returned to Maine on the weekends.

Although I was eager to have Dan in the company, I was also concerned by the problems of succession in other family-owned real estate businesses that I knew well. I had seen and interacted with some terrible examples of sons who had entered their family's businesses and then became undeservedly arrogant and, in effect, damaged the family enterprises. But in Boston Dan proved himself to be a good representative of the family name, as well as a good salesman and manager. As I had expected, since he was the man in the office who bore the Tishman name, clients and potential clients frequently called him, and he had to answer for the company even though he was not in charge of the Boston office.

I kept my ears open and, to my delight, never heard anything bad about what Dan was doing with and for the company in New England. As important, I learned that Dan seemed to like the work, and that his colleagues and clients seemed to like him.

Three years later, Dan agreed to move to our New York offices at 666 Fifth Avenue, and to begin in earnest working up the ladder, eventually reaching the point at which I became confident that he could and should replace me as the firm's leader. He worked almost exclusively in the Construction Management side of the business, leaving the real estate side to the stewardship of my long-time associate, John Vickers.

Once the appropriate successor has come into the company, many family-owned businesses have difficulty in managing the transition between one generation and the next—the older one is reluctant to let go, the younger is overeager to take charge. Fortunately, that did not happen with us. Two sources, I believe, helped ease the transition. The first was the nature of our multifaceted businesses, which enables us rather readily to give ever-larger shares of responsibility to employees on successive jobs.

The second source was my plan for how to transfer my ownership in the company. I felt that so long as I continued to own a controlling interest in the company, even though Dan might have taken the title as CEO he would not really be the company's leader. So, well before I was ready to retire, I transferred the controlling block of stock to him over the course of five years, and the remainder of my stock to Vickers, until I had completely divested myself of any financial interest in the Construction Management company. I made the stock transfers, and have never regretted doing so. I became an employee of my son.

Over the past decade, Dan and his chief associates have surpassed anything I could have imagined for the Tishman firm, aggressively courting and satisfying old and new clients to the point where Tishman Construction became number one in the field in terms of projects and dollar volumes of construction per year. Dan became "Mr. New York City," as the leader of the firm responsible for building the largest and greenest skyscrapers in recent years, and for most of the construction on the various World Trade Center sites, both the publicly and the privately owned. He is the chairman of the Natural Resources Defense Council, a national leader in environmental affairs. Moreover, with his wife, Sheryl, Dan has accepted a role that I could not fill during the many long years of my wife's illness: as a couple they have become an important part of New York's social, charitable, and civic scene.

I believe it is a plus for a client to be able to telephone the man whose name is on the company door. I have been very pleased that at a moment in time when there are no more Fullers in the Fuller Construction firm, or Turners in Turner Construction, that my son Dan, a fourth-generation Tishman, leads the Tishman Construction Company, and that the company continues to be a leader in the field that I pioneered, Construction Management.

# EIGHT

# Charitable and Civic Work

## The Walden Effect

The Walden School, which I attended from kindergarten through graduation from high school, was very progressive and politically ultra-liberal. One lesson from my schooling was an interest in educational innovation.

After Walden, I attended Michigan on an accelerated course, finishing an engineering degree in less than three years.

My college roommate was a year ahead of me and the manager of the football team; when he graduated, he bequeathed me the job. I was happy to have it because it meant that I didn't have to take physical education, which included running up and down the stairs of a stadium grandstand and around an eighteen-hole golf course—not my "thing." This was during the 1944–45 football season, when Michigan had the second-best team in the country, behind Army and its stars Glen Davis and Doc Blanchard, the 1945 Heisman Trophy winner. Since the Michigan football program was quite professional, there wasn't much for a student manager to do to deserve the title of manager; in baseball my assignment would have been dubbed the batboy. However, the job came with a number of off-the-books tasks. One was to scalp tickets for the players and coaches before the games, including at the biggest game of the year, when we played Army at Yankee Stadium. I sold those tickets in my Navy uniform, right in front of my hometown's finest, the New York Police Department. Another task was to "spot" the games for the radio announcer; at Michigan that was Bill Wisner, and at Yankee Stadium, it was the legendary sportscaster Bill Stern.

As I've recounted in an earlier chapter, after leaving the Navy I taught math at Walden. Then came my adventure with Hans Maeder as a founder of the Stockbridge School. Early on, Hans needed financing to purchase the old Mark Hanna estate two miles south of Lenox, Massachusetts, which consisted of a large mansion as well as a huge barn that had been built for Hanna's show horses, as well as the extensive grounds and beautiful forest lands. My uncle David helped Hans and me by introducing us to lenders. We then borrowed enough to purchase the estate from the dissident scholars Scott Buchanan and Carl van Doren, who had taught together at St. John's in Baltimore and had wanted to establish their own college at the Hanna estate. Their teaching method was based on the idea that if you read a certain one thousand books you would learn everything that was required to become an educated person. They had managed to buy the estate but then had fallen out with one another over precisely how to formulate their teaching program. We were happy to take it from there.

By the time I was in my early twenties, then, I was somewhat experienced in charitable affairs, and perhaps more to the point, I accepted that such an involvement was an integral part of living a full and useful life. Later on, when my children began school, my wife and I decided to send them to the New Lincoln School, whose progressive spirit was very similar to that of Walden. A few years further on, I accepted an invitation to serve on the New Lincoln School's board; to do so was part of my obligation not only as a parent but also as a Walden graduate.

One of my fellow board members at New Lincoln was Jack Everett, then the president of the New School for Social Research in Greenwich Village. He asked me to join that university's board; a few days later I was similarly approached by Dorothy Hirshon, chair of that board. She wanted me to understand that the university followed the founders' practice of "pay as you go," which meant that the budget was entirely driven by tuition payments and scholarly grants, leaving very little fund-raising for board members to do. Hirshon and Everett flattered me by saying they wanted me for my educational experience, etc., etc. But I think they also wanted me because by then I had become an experienced hand at putting together charitable dinners.

## Honorary Chairman of the Dinners

By the early 1950s, because of my position in the Tishman Realty and Construction Company, I was regularly sought to raise funds by such organizations as the United Jewish Appeal and the Federation of Jewish Philanthropies, which were then separate entities, as well as the Governor's Committee for Student Scholarships, Carnegie Hall, and other such charities. They wanted me because I could put the touch on the contractors who worked for us. Every city has its own tradition of how money is raised, and in New York the usual practice was to throw a gala dinner and strong-arm your friends, relatives, clients, and especially those to whom you regularly awarded business to buy a table at the dinner. Our contractors were used to having builders ask them to underwrite a table at a dinner for a good cause. Everybody understood the rules of that game.

The first such project that I was asked to do, by Uncle David Tishman, raised an unexpected question for me. David was going to have a room at the New York University Law School named after him, and he had pledged a certain amount of money for it. He wanted me to raise money from our subcontractors to lessen the amount that he would have to pony up. I did it, but I wasn't entirely comfortable doing so. If you're going to have something named after you, shouldn't you contribute all the money for it?

After my "success" with my uncle David's project, just about everybody else in the family tapped me, and so did some of our clients, to raise money for their own commitments. Our subcontractors felt that pressure, but it was difficult for any of them to say "no" to an invitation that bore my name.

Since I had to chair lots of charitable luncheons and dinners, the work of setting up the event, generating the invitations, tracking the replies, etc., became almost a full-time job for some of my colleagues and office staff. I attempted not to chair too many dinners, so as not to exhaust the willingness of our trade contractors and subs to ante up. I contributed what money I could, but in those years, when my elders controlled the family firm, I did not have much in the way of discretionary income. Later, however, when I took over the firm, I would generally contribute first to good causes before twisting the arms of our contractors and suppliers.

Two very liberal, activist lawyers, Lillian Poses and Connie Lindau, were the people behind one of the most interesting of the annual dinners. Their charitable venture was the Mayor's Committee on Scholastic Achievement, and it provided many students with college scholarships.

*At one of the dinners for which I served as chairman, among the honored guests were two close friends, Larry Silverstein and Bill Zeckendorf Jr.*

Begun during the mayoral administration of Robert F. Wagner, Jr., it was continued after he left office in 1965; however, since Wagner's successor John Lindsay would no longer allow them to have an office in City Hall, it was renamed the Governor's Committee and was headquartered elsewhere. The Wagners continued their active association with it.

Lillian Poses was in every way a marvel; one of the earliest women graduates of a law school, she had worked for the Franklin D. Roosevelt Administration until returning to New York after World War II. Just a list of the organizations for which she worked in her later years gives a hint of her breadth and zeal: the Governor's Task Force on Unemployment, the Council Against Poverty, UNESCO, and the International League of Human Rights.

For the Governor's Committee event, I was able to tap all elements of the real estate community, including the top real estate developers, architects, engineers, subcontractors, and the construction trade unions. Harry Van Arsdale, president of the city's Central Labor Council (of unions), was a key ally. Every year, we'd have about a thousand people at a dinner at the Waldorf Hotel, and from them would raise significant sums for student scholarships. I enjoyed working on this dinner, especially because through this event I became very close to Phyllis and Bob Wagner. Phyllis was the widow of publisher Bennett Cerf; after Bennett's death and that of Wagner's wife, Phyllis had married Bob. She and I did many things together; in effect I adopted the Wagners as family, and for many years enjoyed their companionship.

## Progressive Causes

My uncles and cousins in Tishman Realty and Construction were, in general, appalled by my progressive leanings. Within the company my elders repeatedly pilloried me for those leanings. To these uncles, I was a maverick whose actions in the outside sphere horrified them because they were the precise opposite of liberals. But I came by my leanings

*For years, we supported "Camp Central Park," which gave youngsters from inner-city neighborhoods a chance at summer fun.*

legitimately, having been brought up with progressive sympathies from my earliest years and having had those notions continually reinforced by my school, my mother, my Uncle Paul, by various friends—and by what I saw happening around me in life, every day. My progressive upbringing also made me impatient with David and Norman's political opinions, which I heard from them regularly; my uncles were not only conservative, they did not seem to have the same sense of right and wrong as I did. When I would vent about this or that injustice featured in the news, they'd say, "Oh, there you go again," as though whatever I was talking about was either untrue or was meaningless to them. They equated being a progressive with being a Communist. They seemed unable to understand that a person could be progressive without being a Communist, or that if one criticized the way things were being handled in Washington, that did not mean one was not as patriotic as my uncles thought they were.

My habit has always been to put my money where my mouth is. Accordingly, I have always been a contributor to liberal causes and to liberal, even antiestablishment candidates for public office on the local and national scenes. Union leaders knew me as a tough negotiator in work situations, but they also knew that off the site, in regard to political questions I generally stood shoulder-to-shoulder with them. That understanding may have helped them accept my judgments and solutions in jurisdictional disputes.

My uncles and cousins tolerated my liberal impulses because my social and political leanings did not negatively affect the business's bottom line. But that was before the war in Vietnam heated up.

## Antiwar Days

American involvement in the war in Vietnam, a fact since the days of Eisenhower, grew enormously in 1964 under President Lyndon B. Johnson. By 1966 or so, the war had become a quagmire for the United States. I opposed the war, and generally wore a peace symbol. This, of course, drove my uncles up a wall. I wrote letters to important people that I knew, mostly the liberal Democrats such as Senator Robert F. Kennedy, urging them to take stronger public positions that would lead to a cessation of bombing in Vietnam and to de-escalation of the war. In October of 1967, for example, I wrote to several senators, "Simple logic would require every responsible senator holding your opinions to take a positive and vocal stand on this 'number one' issue, and to use every means at your command to persuade your colleagues and the Administration to first cease the bombings and then to withdraw from this conflict." Recently, during the war in Iraq, I found that letter in my files and considered sending it to our current senators, with only a few words changed—principally substituting Iraq for Vietnam.

Vincent McGee, a former Catholic seminary student, was the director of the 6,000-member Business Executives Move for Vietnam Peace, and he became a friend. At the time I met Vinny, in 1969, he had already done something unusual. A few years earlier, upon receiving a draft notice he had decided to protest the war by refusing to be inducted. He didn't attempt to flee to Canada, as many other young men did, or to claim the status of religious conscientious objector. Rather, he publicly burned his draft card in Central Park and allowed himself to be arrested, tried, and convicted. While his case wound its way through the legal system toward the Supreme Court, he worked with the businessmen's group. The New York office was in a cubicle at Random House.

I first met him when he called me for a "loan" to the group to support a mailing. I was willing to put up the money, and almost as a joke asked him to sign a note for it. So I was astonished a month or two later when he came by my office again with a check, a repayment of the loan from the proceeds of the mailing.

I was so impressed that I asked him what I should do next to assist him. He requested that I give a small lunch for friends who were antiwar. I agreed to do that if he could produce two speakers for that lunch, a senator and a retired general. He did, and we had a successful lunch. Then Vinny asked me to co-chair a much larger antiwar lunch gathering, with Random House chief Bennett Cerf as the other co-chair.

As we prepared to set up this event, we understood that it sort of overlapped with the political efforts of New York's mayor at the time, John Lindsay—a Republican liberal who had become a Democrat, due in part to his opposition to the war—to run for president, mostly on an antiwar platform. Senator Frank Church, who was the most visible senatorial opponent of the war, was willing to be our main speaker.

For the lunch to be a successful fund-raiser, there had to be additional prominent co-chairmen who were the leaders of various subgroups that we were trying to tap. But in casting our net for contributions, we later learned, we made an embarrassing mistake—because someone in attendance sent all of the names of the co-chairmen, including mine, to the White House, which later included all the co-chairmen of the event on Nixon's "enemies list."

That list consisted of people against whom the president and his associates planned to take action during his expected second term. Our names made the list solely because we had been willing to listen to Frank Church and Bennett Cerf talk against America's continued involvement in the war! Made public during the Watergate hearings in the summer of 1973, the list became notorious. It also caused ancillary problems, since one of the things that Nixon did was give the list to the IRS, along with an instruction to be especially tough on anyone presumed to be advocating against the president's handling of the war in Vietnam.

As with many of the other people on the Nixon enemies list, I considered my presence on it as a badge of honor. But I was a bit chagrined when the name of my cousin Alan, who had agreed to be a chairman of a real estate industry committee against the war only to assist me—and who was definitely not openly antiwar—was on it as well. But I was relieved when Alan framed the list as it was printed in *The New York Times*, and hung the framed list prominently on his livingroom wall.

By then, Vinny McGee had lost his case in the Supreme Court, and had been sent to Allenwood prison in Pennsylvania for a year. Occasionally I would fly myself and my wife down in my private plane to have lunch with him. He asked me to vouch for him so he could be released on parole, and thereafter, as our private joke, I referred to myself as his parole officer. He would retort that this was not quite accurate, that I was actually his "parole advisor." During Vinny's prison term, as he tells it, he rubbed shoulders with former LBJ aide Bobby Baker, as well as with disgraced politicians like Carmine DeSapio, the Tammany Hall boss convicted for bribery, and with Mafia dons and a former two-star general. In later years, Vinny McGee became the executive director of several foundations that gave tens of millions of dollars for AIDS research and other worthy causes. Vinny always talks openly of his days in opposition to the war in Vietnam, and is quite proud of not having used any means other than legal ones to avoid participating in what he and I believed to have been an obscene war that caused death and destruction for too many people.

## *NYU Medical Center*

New York's welter of great cultural, charitable, and civic organizations offers many opportunities to serve on boards. Many institutions have boards consisting of people who are asked to join principally because they are willing and able to contribute large sums to the institutions. Some boards are very prestigious, and people seek to serve on them to partake of that prestige, to rub shoulders with the stars of culture or with the fabulously wealthy, to belong to a particularly elite inner circle.

That was never of interest to me. I have always tried to serve only on boards where my ideas and active participation can be helpful to the cause or the institution. To be on a board for the prestige associated with it never turned me on; I am also embarrassed and annoyed when I am asked to go on a board simply because of my capacity to donate. If I do join a board for which financial participation is expected, and I then discover that my ideas and experience are not being tapped, I leave the board. There are plenty of other good causes to support.

During the late 1970s and early 1980s, I believed that I could be helpful in the ways that I like to by serving on the board of New York University's medical center, a fine teaching hospital, where we on the board were expected to assist NYU's doctors in obtaining financing for their research and experimental undertakings. My board service there began during the three-year period that we were under the Rockefeller corporate umbrella, and continued after we had emerged as a private company principally owned and led by me.

I enjoyed the NYU Medical Center board meetings. The doctors and their experiments were quite interesting, and I liked hearing about the work from the doctors themselves and contributing my ideas on how to get their projects financed. But during one meeting, after we had listened to such a presentation, a new board member raked the medical investigator over the coals in a nasty and inappropriate way. I seethed, but no one else said anything, so I didn't.

After the meeting, though, I asked the chairman of the university board, "Who is this guy?"

"He's four hundred million dollars," the chairman said.

I then understood 1) that NYU Medical Center was willing to put up with obnoxious behavior from a board member so long as his net worth was substantial and the possibility of obtaining a big donation from him was extant, and 2) that the NYU Medical Center board did not really value me or need me for any intellectual contribution, though I readily contributed financially within my means. I immediately resigned from the board.

## Beginning at The New School

When I resigned from the NYU Medical Center board, I cited other commitments. Primary among them was that I had just gone on the board of The New School for Social Research. Among other things, this new obligation provided me with an opportunity to replace the intellectual stimulation I had initially enjoyed at the NYU Medical Center board. The intellectually stimulating aspect of working with The New School has continued since that moment. As I write this, I have served for almost thirty years on that board, and happily so, as my many years of service there have provided me with the opportunity to "give back" in ideas and in financial contributions to support the goals and principles I had absorbed from my early school days and my experiences as a teacher and a builder. Since joining the board in 1981, I have made The New School a major focus of my time, energy, and resources. I served as chairman of the board for seven years, and for many other years I chaired endless committees and was always a member of the executive committee. It is frequently said that an individual can do a lot for an institution; less frequently said is that an institution can do a lot for someone who becomes closely intertwined with it. The New School has stimulated me in many ways, and continues to do so. My lower and high school teachers, many of whom had connections to The New School and its progressive culture, instilled in me a heritage of progressive views with respect to personal associations, an appreciation of people who are under economic hardships, and the need to be consistent in my support of liberal policies and politicians. The New School was perfect for me in that it combined three of my passions: the progressive tradition, good teaching, and intellectual stimulation.

Recruited by the then-president of The New School, Jack Everett, who was my colleague on the New Lincoln School board, and by its board chairwoman, my good friend Dorothy Hirshon, I joined the board of the Greenwich Village-based university at an interesting moment in its history. Dorothy was a terrific person, and her commitment to the arts, to education, and to those who needed help was tremendous, but in terms of predicting what would be required of me by The New School, she wasn't much of a forecaster.

The New School for Social Research was founded in 1919 as an alternative university, one specifically designed to "educate the educated." In the 1930s, it became "The University in Exile" for the many intellectual refugees from Nazi Germany who resettled in the New York area, and it took on added luster because of these teachers. (In later years, I would honor these teachers, and another individual of their generation and origin, my friend Hans Maeder, by underwriting an annual Hans Maeder lecture at The New School.) From the 1940s through the 1970s, The New School was known primarily for its adult-education classes, held mainly in the evenings, and for having no full-time faculty, only associates who were experts in their field and who taught part-time while they continued to work in their areas of expertise. The structure of the school's classes was also part of the unique design, consisting mostly of small seminars of a dozen or fewer people. The New School boasted of offering a thousand different courses and of giving the students a chance to interact directly with the teachers in and out of the classroom.

Because of this unusual configuration, The New School's board had seen no reason to build up an endowment. Its operation was strictly pay-as-you-go; if enough people did not sign up for a particular course to carry its costs, that course would be canceled before it began. The board would occasionally raise funds for particular projects but not for an endowment.

Before I arrived on the board, The New School had taken over two specialized and highly regarded schools, the Parsons School of Design and the Mannes School of Music, and had branches of these in California and in Paris. As I was arriving, the school was completing the sale of one of its major assets, the "America Today" murals painted by Thomas Hart Benton in 1930-31. The sale raised about $2 million. That money, the first in the school's history to be salted away, constituted its entire endowment.

Selling the murals to fund an endowment was a step in the right direction, but a very small one. Soon after joining the board, I realized three things that I hadn't known before I joined. One, that Jack Everett was leaving as president—a major change in the institution—two, that the school was very nearly bankrupt, and three, that the board was too small and insufficiently affluent to meet the challenge of the university's future financial needs.

## Enlarging the Board and the Horizons

Everett's retirement was not as traumatic for the university as it might have been because he was replaced as president by Jonathan Fanton, a well-respected scholar and administrator who after eighteen years at The New School would go on to lead the John D. and Catherine T. MacArthur Foundation, the source of annual "genius" grants and of major initiatives for education and support for public broadcasting.

When Jonathan visited me in my office at 666 Fifth Avenue, prior to taking up his duties at The New School—the commencement of a

*Ted Kennedy, seen here with his wife, Victoria, in 2000,*
*was honored at The New School.*

long friendship between us—I told him that I was dissatisfied with the size of board as well as its makeup.

The board consisted of twenty-three people. Also, while some board members were philanthropically active within their means, not enough of them had the capacity to give substantially. I suggested expanding the board, and the current board approved the notion, although the university administration advised us that New York State might not do so. Albany did have the power to say no, but they readily approved the expansion of our board from twenty-three to fifty members.

We needed to raise funds, and the university already had an established annual dinner for that purpose, but in recent years the LaGuardia Dinner had become a lackluster affair. I volunteered to assist in this, based on my many years of putting together ceremonial fund-raisers. I helped to expand the list of attendees and of honorees, luring such big names as Senator Ted Kennedy and Chase Manhattan president David Rockefeller as recipients of the annual awards, which succeeded in raising our profile and, with it, our fund-raising.

The most forceful person on the board was Eugene Lang. *Fortune* had celebrated Lang as "the quintessential entrepreneur," and in addition to having made a great deal of money, he had been chairman of the board at his alma mater, Swarthmore. In 1981 Gene established the "I Have a Dream" Foundation, which assisted high school children who dreamed of attending college one day but who did not have the wherewithal. Among Gene's interesting ideas for The New School was to reform and strengthen the undergraduate seminar program so that it would become a regular undergraduate liberal arts college, one that would hold classes during the day and yet retain the small-class-size structure of the adult-education classes. Because of his substantial financial support for that college, and his interest in strengthening it, the board would name it in his honor as the Eugene M. Lang College.

Gene and Jonathan Fanton clashed repeatedly over Lang College, as Gene felt that Jonathan paid most of his attention to the graduate school that had brought luster to The New School for its first sixty years. Part reason for the clash with Gene was Jonathan's understanding of the concomitants of having an undergraduate college—in particular, that The New School would now need to have full-time professors as well as dormitories to house full-time young students, and that fulfilling these obligations would be quite a task. But it was done. The Eugene M. Lang College started with two hundred students; today it has a thousand and is able to compete favorably for interesting and intelligent entering students with neighboring New York University, the country's largest private university.

Since I was the board member most experienced with construction, and since to expand the university we needed new and renovated buildings, one of my first board projects was a dormitory to house some of the undergraduates.

Another of my early projects, even more self-generated, was computerization. I was the first member of the board to own a computer, and I recognized before other board members did how behind the times the school's administration and teaching tools were. My fellow board members were also, shall we say, not computer literate at that time. I pushed for computerization, for instance in the Parsons design school, where the need was most obvious. Today, Parsons, like every other design school, must have software engineers on staff that specialize in computer-aided design. Some educational-policy experts say that if we had not pushed Parsons into the forefront of the field of computer-assisted design in the early 1980s, the school would have seriously fallen behind and would certainly not be the leader in its field that it has become.

I also championed The New School's entry into the field of providing distance-learning courses, as these are an ideal complement to our sort of small-seminar classes in eclectic subjects. Here, too, we were fortunate to be in the forefront of an educational revolution, instead of having to play catch up. Many of our New York area students now take a combination of classroom and distance learning courses.

## *A Controversial Auditorium*

In the 1930s, The New School had built an auditorium, not for classes but for occasional concerts and theatrical performances. The architect, Joseph Urban, a Jewish refugee from Nazi Germany like so many of the other people associated with The New School in that era, had created what was eventually considered to be an art deco masterpiece, with bright vermillion columns on the side walls, and a selection of ascending hues on a series of ceiling projections that added to the feeling of ceiling height. It was a hall, but an intimate one with good sight lines and acoustics. By the 1980s, although designated as a landmark, it had fallen into disrepair. For example, thoughtless maintenance had slopped a single coat of white paint over the scalloped ceiling projections, eroding the architect's original intent.

Jonathan Fanton had presented the board with a list of various "gift opportunities," projects that might interest a board member enough to have him or her want to make a substantial gift with the expectation that the project would afterward bear the donor's name.

I was enthusiastic about the idea of renewing the auditorium where I had often come to hear lectures, mostly on progressive subjects, as far back as my student and teaching days. After our architect did some research on the original design, I suggested that we restore it and I agreed to underwrite the project and to oversee the renovation.

Fanton and I had a number of meetings on the subject of my funding and managing the restoration. One meeting, held in my office, was specifically set for Jonathan to express his concern about the "feature columns" on the side walls and their original bright orange-red (vermilion) color. "It's too garish and I don't like it," Jonathan said, as we sat at my desk. "It will distract the audience from focusing on the stage."

"Look up," I replied. Suspended over my desk was a huge lighting fixture featuring the same bright vermillion that was to be used on the feature columns. The dramatic color did not distract from anything, I argued; in the hall, the vermillion columns merely served as a striking feature, as designed by Rudy Baumfeld, a Viennese architect and

*The auditorium at The New School, originally designed*
*by Joseph Urban and Rudy Baumfeld, which we restored.*

friend of mine, who like Joseph Urban had been schooled in Vienna in the Bauhaus tradition. My demonstration ended the argument.

We redid the hall, including the spectacular stepped ceiling panels, each one a tad lighter than the next, a feature designed so that audience would get the feeling that they were sitting under a much higher ceiling than they were.

During our research for truthfully restoring the auditorium, I learned that when the hall had first opened, a recent architectural school graduate in his first review for *The New Yorker* had written a devastatingly nasty critique of the auditorium. He lambasted every aspect of it, including its shape and location—he ridiculed having an oval-shaped auditorium inside a rectangular building. The young reviewer's name was Philip Johnson, who, after he gave up architectural reviewing, became one of the United States' premier architects. This early diatribe of his, written well before World War II, reflected more than his artistic tastes: it was the result of his sympathy for the Nazis and his then well-known anti-Semitism. My colleagues at The New School, including those on the board, had no inkling of this early, prejudice-based nasty review by Johnson, but I knew about it—and Philip Johnson learned that I knew about it.

The retrofitted auditorium was going to be renamed as the Tishman Auditorium. And perhaps because it was, I decided to invite Philip Johnson to come and have a look at the place before it opened. He no longer wrote architectural criticism, and I hoped that in the more than fifty or so years since his initial review, he would have changed his mind about the original design—or, I should say, about the influence that his own anti-Semitism had had on the critique he had written so long ago. I also knew that many of the recent buildings that had cemented his reputation as a highly respected architect had been commissioned by Jewish clients, such as the Seagram Building in Manhattan.

As I had hoped, Johnson was charmed by the revitalized auditorium, and I believe, embarrassed by his early, unfounded critique of it. As we toured the building, he remarked, "Well, things change." Some on the tour with Phillip were mystified by that remark because they were

*Inducting former Senator Bob Kerrey*
*as president of The New School, May 2002.*

unaware of his early anti-Semitism, but I understood the implications of the sentiment and was happy to hear it directly from Johnson.

The Tishman Auditorium, though small, is beautiful in the subtlety of its design, and is rightfully a New York City landmark. I'm proud to have my family's name on it.

## Bob Kerrey Arrives

After eighteen years, Jonathan Fanton wanted to move on, and was being courted to become the head of the MacArthur Foundation. I was chairman of the board of The New School at the time, and the search for a successor to Jonathan occupied much of the board's time and energies. Realtor Julien Studley, a fellow board member, suggested as our next leader Senator J. Robert Kerrey of Nebraska, who was about to run for a third term. A Medal of Honor recipient for his military

*The New School's newest building, now under construction, is a showcase for environmental design.*

service in Vietnam, in which he lost part of one leg, Bob had been a successful businessman and governor of Nebraska before being elected to the senate. His organizational and management expertise, combined with his natural sympathies for The New School's brand of progressive education, made him a good choice. I asked the board to allow me to stay on as chairman for an additional year, past the six I had already served—the usual maximum for a board chairman—in order to have the honor of installing Bob as our president in 2001 and to help in the transition to his leadership.

We have become friends, Bob and I, and we share some similar traits and passions. One of them is the continued evolution of the university. The New School has a unique history: created to "educate the educated," with adult classes and graduate schools, then having added traditional undergraduate courses and renowned art, fashion, and music schools, and still evolving in terms of courses offered and the make-up of the student body. "We'll never be a traditional school," Kerrey says, and I support that notion. He also calls me his most low-maintenance trustee. I don't know about that.

One of the ideas we completely agree on is for the university to expand its offerings with regard to environmental studies, and to do so rapidly. My intent has been and will be to help the university become a major player in environmental studies, the most important area in which students need to be educated in order to care for the planet properly before it becomes too late to do so. Along those lines, I have immensely enjoyed sponsoring, every summer, a couple of environmental studies students to work with the Alaska Conservation Foundation, in Alaska, on various research and conservation projects. Upon their return to New York, they are required for course credit to give a lecture to the rest of the student body on what they've done over the summer.

The New School's largest environmental teaching opportunity is in the design and construction of our newest building, currently being erected on the southeast corner of Fifth Avenue and 14th Street in Manhattan. It will meet or exceed all current codes and practices for environmentally friendly or "green" buildings, and will be a showcase for the use of such designs and innovations in academic and commercial buildings.

## *Museum for African Art*

The Museum for African Art, in New York, was founded a quarter-century ago.

It is quite unusual in that it has no substantial collections of its own. Its primary purpose has always been to assemble and arrange African art collections from many sources and place them in a variety of well-known museums around the world. I knew of it from afar because of my continuing interest in African art gained by my stewardship of the Paul and Ruth Tishman African art collection that Disney bought at my insistence, and eventually donated to the Smithsonian Institution.

In the Museum for African Art's first decades I was not involved with it, but then the museum acquired a site on which to build at the edge of Harlem, at 110th Street and Fifth Avenue. I considered that site one of the best in the city for its purposes, allowing it to be the first museum on what is known as New York's "Museum Mile" that runs down Fifth Avenue from 110th and includes the Metropolitan, the Guggenheim, the Jewish Museum, The Museum of the City of New York, the Cooper-Hewitt design museum, and others. But there were many problems with the 110th Street site. It had been more-or-less empty for many years—I say so because it was the location of some community vegetable gardens while awaiting use as a building site. Another problem was that part of the site was owned by the museum, part by the City of New York, and part by a private entity called the Edison Schools.

The original plan for constructing a building on the site called for part of that building to become an Edison school while the rest would be used for the museum. That combination became untenable when Edison Schools flirted with bankruptcy and were forced to give up their portion of the site to the city. The community gardeners then made a fuss because they did not want to lose their favorite mini-farms. Negotiations between the city and the museum were thus quite complicated and took two years to resolve.

Most of this tussle had taken place before I became involved, and when I did become involved it was because the museum wanted some volunteer—meaning "free"—help. The board of the museum had commissioned renowned architect Bernard Tschumi, dean of architecture at Columbia University, to design its future building. When Tschumi's plans came in, Jonathan D. Green, as co-chairman of the museum's board, asked me to look them over. Jonathan, president of Rockefeller Center Construction, had once been my boss when Tishman Construction had been a Rockefeller subsidiary, and was a long-time friend.

It was a familiar role for me to look over an architect's plans to see whether or not they were realistic. I quickly noted that in Tschumi's attempt to make the museum look African, he had suggested featuring wood on the exterior. To me, this was a fatally flawed idea; I pointed out that the wood would deteriorate in a short time from direct exposure to the sun and New York's harsh winters, and that it would be impossible to maintain. Tschumi disagreed. He did not want to change his wood façade design, claiming this was his artistic vision and should be accepted. We wrangled with him for a while, but eventually reached an impasse. At this point, the museum, which was then facing an entirely new development and financing scheme as well as a radical new site configuration, decided to engage a different architect. But who should that architect be? I recommended the dean of architecture at Yale, Robert A. M. Stern.

I've taken a bit of ribbing for suggesting the exchange of the dean of one Ivy League architecture school with the dean of another Ivy League architectural school, but the decision was ratified when Stern created an excellent and much more practical design.

The museum had devised an interesting way to deal with the capital costs of land and building: a substantial part of the site would be created as high-rise, condominium apartments, physically integrated with the museum on the lower levels, and sharing development and on-going maintenance costs.

A major coup for the museum, as the foundations of the building were proceeding, was to secure the participation of The Nelson Mandela Center for Memory and Dialogue. Seated within the Museum will be a Mandela Center that will be a major part of the museum's educational activities and outreach.

# On Being a Lucky Man

When I look back on my career, I am proud of what I have done, particularly in initiating the methodology of Construction Management and practicing it as a profession. I am also fully aware that I have been incredibly lucky.

I don't mean lucky in the same sense as someone who wins the lottery. Rather, I have been lucky in that life has presented me with challenging and extraordinary opportunities—it presents everyone with opportunities—and that I was situated in places, ways, and habits of mind that allowed me to take advantage of the opportunities that came my way.

Early on, I went with the flow. I emerged from college and from my stint in the Navy without a fixed career in mind; I thought I would do something involving electrical engineering, my major during college, and only drifted into teaching at the Walden School as a temporary measure. I had no plan in life. It had not occurred to me that I should consider joining Tishman Realty & Construction. My father, who had been in that firm, had died long ago, and I knew very little about the firm or the business other than what I picked up through my friendship with Uncle Paul, whom I admired not so much for his occupation—I hardly knew about that—as for his liberal politics and his enthusiasms for photography, woodworking, and dogs, enthusiasms that I shared.

When Uncle David sought to bring me into the firm in 1947, his pitch was not one that made me feel particularly wanted or comfortable. The gist of it was that, as he said, he "couldn't see a Tishman graduate as an engineer and not in the firm." A backhanded invitation. Nonetheless I joined, anticipating that I would be apprenticed to Paul and that this would be wonderful. I hadn't realized that Paul was on his way out of the firm, nor that I would be at a distinct disadvantage in the family firm when compared to my cousins, because I had no father as sponsor and advocate.

Not having a father in the firm to advocate for me, however, produced my first lucky break. I was assigned to construction, which David and his brothers then considered the least important aspect of their real estate business. Another lucky thing was that the particular set of cousins about my age, in the business, relied on their familial connections for their potential advancement, not on their native abilities. I had to make my own way, which had its own rewards, and perhaps also made me more acceptable to the non-Tishman employees. My cousins seemed to be more aware of competing with me than I was of the need to compete with them.

A third lucky instance, in these early years, was occasioned by the firm's palpable need for someone to take charge of construction as a consequence of there being many new Tishman buildings to be constructed in the postwar boom. When Paul departed the firm, his former lieutenant Joe Blitz was put in charge of construction, but Blitz soon left to join Paul, creating a vacuum of leadership in construction that I was able to fill. By the time I was twenty-five and heading to the altar to marry Susan, in 1951, I was in charge of construction on the huge Ivy Hill housing project in New Jersey.

I was also tremendously lucky in the sequence, size, and prominence of the building projects that arose while I was in the family-run public company. By 1965, I had already been in charge of a number of substantial buildings for the public company's portfolio, Tishman Realty and Construction reached out in a new direction, with the partnership that created the new Madison Square Garden and Two Penn Plaza. This opportunity to build for someone other than my family, yet to build in the same spirit of "owner/builder" that we had used in the past, was another lucky break for me, as it set me on the path to a future separate and apart from my family. For the next dozen years, before the public Tishman Company was folded and its assets sold off, my construction division acted as construction managers for others as well as for our family.

It was from this background that the professional field of Construction Management emerged. The basic idea of Construction Management is to manage the construction of a client's project as though you are the client's own internal construction department. At the time of the first project that we supervised for owners other than Tishman Realty, I considered the idea to be logical and imperative, although somewhat revolutionary. I believed it should be how construction was done on large projects, and thought of it as a sales edge for our company. Indeed, it was, as we could tout CM to clients and point to it as why we were going to be better for them than, say, a large conventional general contractor firm. My consistent ability to sell owner clients on the idea that we would be working for them in the manner of a lawyer or an architect, on a professional basis provided a marketing edge for Tishman Construction. Henry Ford, Jr., for one important instance, understood the idea at once, and it was the basis for his engaging us to be the Construction Manager for the Renaissance Center in Detroit, and for the other owners on the very large projects that followed. The alacrity with which such large and important clients took to the idea of Construction Management was based not only on how it would save them money and aggravation, but also on the professionalism of the service we would render. Their acceptance of CM gave to me, and to other prospective purveyors, the understanding that CM ought to replace general contracting for all future sizable projects, and, that, in effect, began the modern field of Construction Management.

There may be some truth to the old adage that "You make your own luck." There were lucky consequences for me in the breakup of the old Tishman Realty and Construction firm, in 1977. My family and our major outside stockholders had decided that the need was to get rid of the former public company because it was hampering the partners' ability to make the sort of large personal, after-tax profit from real estate that our privately held competitors were making. The breakup would also be an occasion to sell the company's portfolio of buildings, and for each of the three divisions to go out on its own, the development part under Bob Tishman and his son-in-law Jerry Speyer, the management part under Bob's brother Alan, and the construction division, under my leadership. That separation not only suited me fine, it was a lucky break for me, because in the ensuing three years under the Rockefeller Center umbrella, the operation I headed up was able to make an easy transition from being part of a public company to being fully on our own.

Having insisted on retaining the Tishman company name and history, I took advantage of the opportunity that afforded me to tell potential clients about all the buildings we had constructed for the family, and how my colleagues and I would bring that expertise to bear on their behalf, as Construction Manager on their construction projects. I knew that I had some of the best construction management experts in the business as colleagues, and was delighted at being able to tout that, as well, to potential clients. After all, I could say to potential clients, these are the men who acted as Construction Managers for the three tallest buildings in the world.

Luck was also involved in our landing the assignment as Construction Manager on the reconstruction of a Disney World side hotel while waiting for a favorable economic climate in which to begin the EPCOT construction; when the need came up for Disney to have another hotel built, and Disney's own executives and internal construction people were busy on other projects. When I spoke up and asked if our firm could be permitted to develop that hotel, they were more than willing to entertain the proposition. I had never personally developed a property, but the Disney executives knew of my many years of work in the family development firm, where I had been involved in all major decisions about development, and that, coupled with the work we were doing for Disney in Construction Management, allowed them to feel comfortable in awarding me the opportunity to develop our first hotel.

Luck is also timing, and that was never truer than in this instance. Because the Rockefeller interests did not want to be in the development business for anyone other than that family, when this Disney-related hotel project came along, in conjunction with internal Rockefeller family pressure to reorganize their interests, it made economic sense for them to encourage me and my colleagues to buy out their interest after three years, and on very friendly terms, and for each entity to go its separate ways. The Rockefeller interests knew the hotel would be good for us—an extra assurance, for them, that we would be able to pay them the $6.5 million price set on the construction division.

At several points in the ensuing years, Tishman Construction had the opportunity to function as a general contractor rather than as a Construction Manager—and I chose not to pursue the GC path, even though in opting to be only a CM we gave up the opportunity to now and then make a great deal of money from a particular project. What we were obtaining in exchange, I was very aware, was much lower risk accompanied by the ability to reap a consistent and comfortable living from our fees. Functioning as a CM instead of a GC also enabled us to work on many more projects than we might have been awarded as a GC. As the business cycles went up and down, and as Tishman Construction continued to prosper and to remain independent and privately owned, I felt vindicated in the decisions that I had made.

Luck was also on my side in sending me John Vickers, a sensitive and most talented individual who started with Tishman Construction as a summer intern while he attended Columbia University's business school, and has been a colleague ever since. John has become a recognized and highly regarded leader in the hotel industry. Another stroke of luck was finding, in my son Dan, a successor who through diligence, personal charm and great business sense has taken Tishman Construction to new heights. A decade after I turned over the business to Dan, his top echelon of executives, I am proud to say, still consists mainly of those who had been colleagues of mine at Tishman Construction for many years during my watch.

Blessed with such exceptionally talented and loyal colleagues, I never shied away from seizing the opportunities that luck presented. Those opportunities made it possible for our firm to achieve what I consider my greatest accomplishment, the transformation of the methodology for coordinating and supervising large-scale construction projects, elevating what had been a master tradesman's craft to being the *profession* of Construction Management, a discipline now taught in hundreds of universities, and practiced on just about every major construction project throughout the world.

• • •

As this book was nearing completion, Tishman Construction was sold to and merged with Aecom, a publicly-held company that is one of the largest and most respected providers of professional, technical and management support services in the world ... formed from many of the world's finest engineering, design, environmental, and planning companies. For me, the merger is bittersweet. Sweet, in that it will enable Dan and my former colleagues and friends of many years, to become the Tishman Construction Division of Aecom, and thus, even larger players in major construction projects throughout the world. Bitter, because after all that I had worked hard to create, build, and preserve as an independent company with a rich heritage, Tishman Construction will no longer be private nor independent.

I now carry the title of "Chairman Emeritus" and will continue to watch, with pride, the work of my former colleagues under their new flag. Now 85 years of age, I suppose it is to be expected and appropriate that I would retire, but the desire to be in the arena, immersed in the action, I am discovering, does not entirely fade with age. I must admit the thrill of *"Building Tall"* still remains.